Endorsements

This book comes at a time when   lf
within the global economy. China   al
development is crucial. This book   his
process and Chi Lo should be a

~ *Nick Lord, ~~~~*   *tor,*
FinanceAsia.

This extraordinary forward-looking book condenses complex economic issues into concise arguments for understanding Asia's economic future under the threat of China's economic dominance. It refutes many conventional perceptions about China and Asia and instigates thinking outside the box. I do not agree with all its assessments, but this is precisely why I want to read this book.

~ *Edward Lo, Senior Account Manager,*
NEC Hong Kong Ltd.

In this provocative book, Chi Lo goes beyond earlier diagnoses of what caused the '97–'98 Asian financial crisis and offers a penetrating look at the challenges and opportunities ahead. In a straight-forward style, he examines what China's rise will mean for a region beset with massive overcapacity and shoddy corporate governance.

~ *Paul Wiseman, Asia Correspondent,*
USA Today.

This is a remarkable book on the critical issues of drastic economic development in Asia. Will China be the economic leader of the world in the 21st century? Chi's book provides distinct facts and analysis on China's future economic development in Asia. It is up to us to reveal the answer after reading this masterpiece.

~ *Dr. Daniel Cheung, Associate Professor, Banking and Finance,*
School of Business and Administration, The Open University of Hong Kong.

When Asia Meets China in the New Millennium

China's Role in Shaping Asia's Post-Crisis Economic Transformation

Chi Lo

PEARSON
Prentice
Hall

Singapore London New York Toronto Sydney Tokyo Madrid
Mexico City Munich Paris Capetown Hong Kong Montreal

Published in 2003 by
Prentice Hall
Pearson Education Asia Pte Ltd
23/25 First Lok Yang Road
Singapore 629733

Pearson Education offices in Asia: *Bangkok, Beijing, Hong Kong, Jakarta, Kuala Lumpur, Manila, New Delhi, Seoul, Shanghai, Singapore, Taipei, Tokyo*

Printed in Singapore

5   4   3   2   1
06   05   04   03

ISBN 0-13-102842-1

Contents

About the Author   vii

Preface   ix

Introduction: Asia – The Beginning or the End?   1

Chapter 1 It is More Than a Currency Crisis   6
    Setting the Scene   7
    The Missing Pieces   10
    The Financial Culprit   14
    Moral Hazard   19
    Self-Fulfilling Pessimism   21

Chapter 2 Asia Cheats on Reforms   25
    Acknowledging the Changes   26
    Illusive Healing   30
    Structural Flaws   38
    Global Equilibrium Upset   47

Chapter 3 China Shapes the New Economic Paradigm   50
    Debt Deflation: Troubles Ahead   51
    Formidable China   53
    Pressuring Asia   58
    Engine for Growth and Investment   63
    Push for Reform and Cooperation   66

Chapter 4 Foreign Trade and Investment –
    The Chinese Magnet   70
    No Chinese Thief   70
    What's Right and What's Wrong?   79
    Walking a Fine Line   83
    The Chinese Magnet and Southeast Asia   87

Chapter 5 Changing Fortunes Between the Yen and
    the Renminbi   92
    Japan's Fading Glory   93
    The Japanese Burden   98
    China's Rising Influence   105
    The Yen Loses Its Shine in Asia   110

Chapter 6 Case Study 1 – China's Pressure on Hong Kong 117
    Double Whammy   118
    Structural Woes   120
    What Kills Confidence?   123
    Erosion of a Traditional Role   129
    Surviving the Challenges   135

Chapter 7 Case Study 2 – China's Pressure on Taiwan   140
Liquidity Trap is Not the Worst Problem   141
Bad Banks and Debt Trap   144
Rubbing Salt into the Wound   150
The China Squeeze   152
A Secular Downtrend   156

Chapter 8 The Big Picture and the New Paradigm   160
A Global Problem   161
The Evil Combination   165
A New Pricing Game   168
More Productivity, Less Profits   172
Asia's New Economic Model   174
China – A Threat, a Catalyst, or What?   177

Index   185

About the Author

Chi Lo, enlisted as a member of the International Who's Who Professionals in 2000, is an economic strategist based in Hong Kong. Prior to his consulting practice, he was Research Director (Greater China) at banking giant HSBC and Chief Economist (Northeast Asia) at Standard Chartered Bank in Hong Kong. He has over 15 years of international research experience in economics, financial markets, and public policy and standards development, covering North American and Asian economies.

Before returning to Asia in 1996, he served as Economic Advisor at the federal deposit insurance agency under the Canadian Government Department of Finance in Ottawa, Canada. He also worked at financial regulatory agencies and blue chip investment banks in the UK, US, Canada, Singapore, and Hong Kong.

He has published widely in international periodicals and newspapers, including *The Wall Street Journal*, *Far Eastern Economic Review*, and *Finance Asia*, and frequently appears as a guest speaker on CNN, CNBC, Reuters, Bloomberg, and the BBC.

Chi Lo taught applied economics and banking and finance courses at several universities' departments of professional and continuing education. He is also a frequent guest speaker at classes of EMBAs, MBAs, and Finance Diplomas of various universities in Asia and North America, and at international seminars, such as the Asian Development Bank and United Nations conferences.

Preface

The 1997/1998 Asian financial crisis has received thorough research and discussion in the business economics literature. But the economic outlook and difficulties due to structural changes in Asia after the regional debacle have yet to receive the sufficient analysis and discussion that they deserve. While everyone is talking about the emerging economic power of China and is excited about her entry into the World Trade Organisation, there has been no systematic discussion about China's role in Asia's post-crisis economic restructuring. Crucially, insufficient effort has been made to link the structural changes in the global economy to Asia's economic transformation.

This book aims at tackling these issues by discussing the inter-reactions between all key global, regional, and local economic forces in Asia's structural changes after the 1997/1998 regional crisis. In economics, this is called a General Equilibrium Approach. The discussion also highlights the influence of China's economic clout in driving regional development into a new economic paradigm of intensifying competition, eroding pricing power, profit squeezing, and constraining economic growth. However, due to the extensiveness and complexity of this subject, only a comprehensive coverage is provided on the critical issues and economic trends that will be unfolding in the early part of this century. No attempt is made to evaluate these complicated forces exhaustively.

The discussions use macroeconomic concepts to analyse real-life business and market events, and to project the advent of a new economic era in Asia. There are anecdotes for Asia's reform success, but there are also anecdotes to show Asia's reform deficiency. This lack of conviction is precisely the problem in Asia's reform process. The anecdotes are conflicting and they do not add up to the observed macroeconomic trends. This gap between the micro and macro observations is a major source of concern that this book is trying to address.

Real-world examples, including case studies and corporate examples, are used to support the arguments and projected trends in the book. Each chapter has a theme of its own. But these individual chapters are indeed building blocks that add up to the main theme of Asia's economic transformation under the shadow of China and the changing global economy. Readers will find continuity as they read through the book. But they will also find stand-alone thematic discussions of real-world events in the individual chapters without feeling lost.

Many of the issues discussed herein are controversial and open-ended, and as such there are no right or wrong answers. The purpose of this book is to stimulate critical thinking to further readers' understanding of the regional and global market conditions. A critical approach is adopted, questioning conventional wisdom at times, to assess and analyse Asia's development after the 1997/1998 financial crisis and to project its outlook in the new economic paradigm.

Financial market practitioners, corporate executives, government advisors, and students seeking to understand Asia's economic and financial development should find this book particularly useful for brainstorming and developing business and policy strategies.

All economic data, data estimates and charts used in this book are based on the data bank provided by CEIC Data Company Ltd., unless stated otherwise in the text. CEIC is an information services company, based in Hong Kong with strategic presence throughout Asia, engaged in providing time-series macroeconomic data on Asian and other major economies. It sources the data from national governments, government agencies and the Standard and Poor's Group. The latter has been a strategic ally with CEIC since 1995. The Asian database consists of over 100,000 raw data series and covers 15 countries.

Introduction

Asia – The Beginning or the End?

There are the disappointed. Notably, many foreign investors have expected Asia to come out of the 1997/1998 Asian financial crisis with strong economic reforms to transform the region into a more amiable investment destination. Economists, policy advisors, and progressive officials have expected their post-crisis reform policy prescriptions to be implemented, elevating Asia into a better socioeconomic environment.

In particular, the region needs to implement structural reforms to strengthen its banking and corporate sectors. These changes include not only recapitalising the banks, but also uprooting their policy lending role, cutting bad debts, increasing market discipline for monitoring lending practices, improving bank and corporate transparency, accountability and management, and purging cronyism. The corporates also need to cut their huge debt burden, change their short-sighted, quick-profit trading practices, and focus on long-term profitability and efficiency. Asia as a whole needs to shift from the low-efficiency, manufacturing-based, export-oriented economic model to a high value-added, service-based, consumption-oriented model.

Unfortunately, most Asian governments have missed the opportunity to restructure their economies thoroughly. Despite a robust economic rebound in the two years after the 1997/1998 debacle, which should provide the necessary macroeconomic support for implementing reforms, many regional governments still lack the will to bite the bullet. Some have slipped on reform, while others have even cheated on reform. All this represents a big blow to the expectations and confidence in Asia's future.

However, these are not all the problems that Asia will face in the coming years. There will be more disappointment for optimists. Insufficient reforms mean that some of the economic problems that led to Asia's financial crisis have remained. These problems will be a major drag on Asia's growth for many years. They will also be the major obstacles to the region's economic restructuring under an increasingly competitive global environment and a rising economic giant, China.

Then there are those optimists who still hope that Japan will soon rebound from her economic quagmire and become a powerhouse in Asia, leading the region in its economic changes. They will likely be disappointed again, as they have been in the past ten years. Japan will eventually reform. The bad news is that it will take more than a decade of uncertainty for Japan to reach its pinnacle. Japan's inability to reform will keep her as a lost economic power in Asia in the new economic paradigm. More crucially, the loss of Japan as a major demand source for global exporters, due to her economic weakness, will add deflationary pressures to the global system. This will, in turn, make Asia's economic transformation tougher than it would have been if Japan were a stronger economic force.

On the other hand, China's rise in economic clout will complicate the economic and financial trends that will unfold in the years ahead. On the positive side, the Mainland could be a major force driving Asia's income and investment growth in the long-term. She could even replace the US and Japan as the most important economy for Asia. The Chinese renminbi would emerge as a major regional currency. Its status would rival that of the Japanese yen in influencing Asia's economic stability.

However, before Asia realises the economic benefits, China's rising competitiveness, and resolve to get ahead and potential success in reform could inflict significant economic pains in Asia's road to rejuvenation. Asian economies that fail to change would likely be marginalised by China. Even the lowest-cost producers could be eliminated. The persistence of these economic pains will surprise many because the breadth and depth of these unfolding forces have not been seen before. In particular, Asia is entering a new economic paradigm of rising competition, weak pricing power, and slow economic growth.

In effect, this new paradigm emerges partly as a result of the economic transformation that Asia will eventually go through after the bursting of its economic bubble in 1997/1998. It also arises partly because of the rising economic might of China in the global economy. The transformation involves the daunting task of revamping Asia's economic structure to survive in an integrated world economy. The China factor highlights the economic hostility and the formidable challenge that Asia is facing due to the competitive stress inflicted by the Middle Kingdom in the regional environment. Meanwhile, there is little hope that Japan will revive her economic influence to balance China's influence. Japan will likely remain a lost economic power in the early stage of the new economic era.

That is not to say that it would be all smooth-sailing for China. The Mainland also faces daunting challenges itself, but this is not the focus of the book. China's emergence as a pressing force in Asia going forward stems from my view of positive reform dynamics. There are, of course, those who have a negative reform view on China, that her reform process, and the economy, would collapse in a few years. I will address this issue in the conclusion of this book. However, it is without a doubt that China will be a major economic force shaping Asia's economic changes in the years ahead — whether China thrives or collapses.

To survive the new economic paradigm, Asia will have to revamp its traditional manufacturing- and export-based economic model to a high value-added and consumption-based model. However, as old habits die hard, there is no clear sign yet that the regional governments have the resolve to revamp their old and outdated economic systems. The process of uprooting cronyism is especially disappointing. Unless the authorities get back on track to tough reforms, the onset of this new economic era will be a very painful experience under China's economic shadow.

Thus, long gone are the good old days of fast economic growth and easy money made from surging asset prices. The excess capacity overhang that Asia inherited from the investment bubble before 1997 and insufficient reform after the crisis will combine to erode manfacturers' pricing power and profit growth for a long time. What follows in the coming years in Asia will likely be a prolonged period of disinflation, with periods of deflationary traps. Robust demand that existed in the early and mid-1990s will not return anytime soon. All this will lead to chronic weakness in some Asian asset prices and currencies. How the new paradigm will unfold depends on how the regional governments' economic and structural policies will evolve.

However, there is no reason to believe that China could harm Asia, for example, by gaining export market share and foreign investment at the expense of the rest of the region. In the new economic era, some Asian neighbours will inevitably see China's economic success as a threat to their security. But this "Chinese fear" could also turn out to be a major incentive to spur Asia's reform efforts if the region wants to strengthen itself to meet the Chinese challenge.

The plan of the book is as follows.

Chapter 1 sets the scene for discussing China's role in shaping Asia's economic transformation with a brief account of the Asian 1997/1998 crisis. A critical approach is taken rather than a conventional analysis of what had happened because the causes and impact of the crisis have been well-documented.

Chapter 2 argues that despite the painful experience of the crisis, Asia had cheated on reforms. It highlights the problem that anecdotal evidence for reform success does not add up to observed macro trends that show the lack of reform. This lack of conviction for reform bodes an uncertain future for Asia's economic development because the global environment is worsening. The regional governments' lip service to reform has sown the seed for more economic pains as the region goes through a post-bubble economic transformation.

Chapter 3 discusses the global forces behind the emergence of a new economic paradigm and highlights China's role in driving the changing dynamics of trade, competition, investment, and growth in Asia. I refute the conventional view that the deteriorating Asian trade environment could push the Chinese to devalue their currency. I also argue against the view that China has gained export market share and foreign investment at the expense of the rest of Asia.

Chapter 4 follows from Chapter 3's discussion on foreign investment flows into Asia. It looks at China's rise as the magnet for foreign investment and as a major player in international trade. I will argue against the notion that China's currency devaluation in 1994 was the foundation for the Asian crisis, and defuse the concern that China would displace the rest of Asia by continuing to gain foreign trade and investment shares. The focus is on what China has done right and what most Asian economies, especially Japan, have done wrong to deserve the differing votes of investor confidence.

Chapter 5 extends the analysis to argue that China would overtake Japan as Asia's economic powerhouse. The Chinese renminbi would be more crucial than the Japanese yen in affecting Asia's systemic stability in the coming years. In particular, I argue that the impact of the yen on other Asian economies has diminished sharply, and that this phenomenon would continue in the new economic era as Japan would remain a lost economic power for many years.

Chapter 6 and 7 are case studies, looking at China's pressure on Hong Kong and Taiwan, two Asian tiger economies that are also part of the Greater China economy. They serve as a wake-up call to those who think strong economic fundamentals will allow an economy to be complacent and avoid painful economic reforms. The two case studies also highlight the risk that both Hong Kong and Taiwan could be stuck in a secular downtrend, despite the perception that they should be spared the Chinese stress due to their integration with the Mainland's economy.

Chapter 8 concludes the analysis by looking at the long-term economic and structural forces behind the global demand constraint. Insufficient demand will reinforce excess capacity and the China competitive stress to pressure Asia in its transformation in the new economic paradigm. I argue that Asia's traditional asset-trading, export-led economic model would become obsolete. It will have to revamp itself to focus on brand-building and domestic-oriented activities. The discussion ends with a note on China's ability to ignite changes and how so many so-called "China experts" can get their readings wrong on China.

Chapter 1

It is More Than a Currency Crisis

Let us start by thinking the unthinkable. Imagine it is 2030 in Asia, the Chinese economy is rivalling that of the US to become the largest in the world. Chinese exports constitute more than one-quarter of the world's total, surpassing Japan, North America, and Europe. An average Chinese earns over US$40,000 a year, compared to only US$900 in 2000. China is also the biggest export market for Asia, followed by the US, Japan, and Europe. There are Chinese company headquarters in all major cities in the world, with Chinese firms and factories employing millions of fellow Asians in the region.

Mandarin is the major regional business language in Asia and the Chinese currency, the renminbi, replaces the Japanese yen as the key regional currency for international trade. In addition to Chinese goods, Chinese services, movies, music, and fashion have also penetrated every corner of Asia. Thriving together with China is the Asian regional economies, whose average income has jumped thirty fold from 2000.

Meanwhile, the competitive pressure from the Mainland has pushed Southeast Asia into what resembles an economic union to exploit economies of scale to survive. East Asia has formed a free trade block, spanning from Japan to Indonesia, countering the North American Free Trade Area and the Euroland. Meanwhile, at the southeast corner of the region, Malaysia and Singapore, which were separated in 1965 when Singapore became an independent city-state, have reunited, at least economically. In the Malaysian–Singaporean union, like the 11 European states that merged to form Euroland in 1999, Singaporeans are able to invest, work, and live anywhere in Malaysia and vice versa. There is free trade and a common currency underpinned by common economic policies in the two economies.

Now back to reality. Of course, projecting long-term growth is not for the fainthearted. It is especially difficult to forecast China's outlook, given the complexity of her political and economic growth dynamics. The idea of a Southeast Asia economic union may also seem hypothetical, farfetched, and even undesirable to many. But when governments are scrambling to remain competitive in the face of a rising economic giant, China, thinking out of the box commands a premium. Further, the above outlook in the next three decades or so is only one of many possible outcomes that involve China's role in shaping Asia's future economic development. The Middle Kingdom could turn out to be a rogue country, or collapse within a few years, as some pessimists see, sending seismic waves across the globe, sinking the Asian region in no time.

However, it is not the interest of this book to project the pessimistic extreme. It is far more crucial to examine China's role as a catalyst to bring about changes and create a potential win-win outcome for Asia. This is because the rise of China's economic might is emitting powerful forces, especially after the Asian crisis in 1997/1998, in shaping Asia's economic future. In other words, a new economic paradigm is emerging, with China as the major driving force behind it. The defining characteristics of the new economic era will include abundance of cheap consumer goods, constrained economic growth, persistent weak pricing power, profit squeeze on manufacturers, and rising competition. Even if our positive story depicted above plays out, it will not be smooth-sailing for Asia because the competitive power of China will act both as a threat and an opportunity to Asia's well-being.

Setting the Scene

To set the scene for our theme discussion of the role of China in shaping a new economic model in Asia, let us look at the

1997/1998 Asian crisis again. The debacle not only exposed the region's structural weakness, it also unleashed Asia's chronic excess supply capacity into the global market. The inability of the regional governments to implement sweeping reforms to rid the region of its economic and structural woes after the financial crisis has put in place a painful transition towards the new economic future. I shall take a critical approach rather than a conventional analysis of what had happened because the causes and impact of the crisis have been well-documented.

In the period between 1965 and 1996, East Asia's annual income per person grew by 5.5% a year. That was more than double the growth rate of the developed world, and contrasted sharply with the chronic income contraction in Africa and the Middle East during the same 30-year period. Following the early economic success of Japan in the 1970s, Asia's four "tiger" economies – Hong Kong, Taiwan, South Korea and Singapore – succeeded the Japanese as the major economic stars, delivering most of Asia's growth miracle in the 1980s and 1990s. An average citizen in the four "tiger" economies made more than US$20,000 a year between 1970 and 1996, compared with an average of just US$6,500 in other Southeast Asian economies.

Though a laggard in absolute income levels, the Southeast Asian economies, notably Thailand, Indonesia, and Malaysia (or the "TIM" economies, which represented the most dynamic economies in East Asia outside the "tiger" region before the Asian crisis) did not do too badly in terms of income growth. Their average income jumped by more than four times between 1970 and 1996. The "tiger" and "TIM" economies shared a set of common factors that enabled their remarkable performance. These factors include export-oriented and pro-market economic policies, supported by macroeconomic stability, agricultural reform, financial liberalisation, and industrial policies designed to encourage technological growth.

Against this background, it is thus surprising to see the eruption of the regional crisis in July 1997, with a scale and depth that shocked even the die-hard pessimists of Asia. With the benefit of hindsight, while one can generally attribute the crisis to a combination of external sector woes, rotten domestic financial systems, regulatory inadequacy, inappropriate financial liberalisation, and loss of investor confidence, the vulnerability of some of the Asian economies to crisis infection is still puzzling.

It is understandable that the "TIM" economies suffered as a group due to their geographical proximity and close economic linkages. They had similar production structures, focusing on mid- to low-end consumer products and electronics, and they competed directly with each other for export market shares. They even had similar structural problems, such as broken banking systems and poor regulatory frameworks. However, some of the other crisis-hit economies had little connection with the centre of the financial shock in Southeast Asia. They also had very different financial systems and, by many measures, had better economic fundamentals than Southeast Asia in general.

For example, South Korea, Taiwan, and Hong Kong are far from the origin of the regional crisis. They have only limited direct economic linkages with the southeast. They also have different production structures, having long been graduated from the highly labour intensive products that still dominate most of the Southeast Asian exports. Last but not least, before the crisis, the Northeast Asian economies, notably Hong Kong and Taiwan, had much stronger economic fundamentals than most of the Southeast Asian economies. Taiwan, South Korea, and China also had capital controls that restricted hot money flows.

How, then, did the Southeast Asian crisis virus infect Northeast Asia? Why did the whole of East Asia sink despite these systemic and economic diversities between the north and the south? All this leads to an inevitable corollary that the Asian crisis was more than a simple currency crisis. Of course, individual Asian economies suffered their own currency crises in 1997 and 1998 and the usual symptom of excessive speculation attacking the markets was present. But there must be some common thread that linked the regional economies together so that when a shock occurred in one of them, a domino effect followed disregarding their systemic and economic differences.

A deeper look suggests that the currency crises were only part of a broader problem of a financial crisis featured by a combination of vested interests sabotaging public interest (or moral hazard as it is known in economics; see further discussion below), poor regulatory systems, crony capitalism, and asset bubbles. These weaknesses were both structural and fundamental in nature, causing major economic problems to erupt when the maximum stress point was reached. Notably, the problems impaired the ability of the economy's financial system to serve as an effective intermediary for capital allocation between savers and investors. When savings and investment decisions were distorted, a financial crisis became inevitable.

The Missing Pieces

The catalyst that exposed these financial fault lines and shattered investor confidence was external sector weaknesses stemming from prolonged domestic savings and investment imbalance. Excessive investment over domestic savings in the decade leading up to the Asian crisis had led to excessive demand outstripping supply in the Asian economies. This, in turn, created excessive imports of goods and services over exports, i.e., a current account deficit.[1]

A large current account deficit is a dangerous economic signal reflecting that the economy is spending beyond its means. This, in turn, means that the economy would have to rely on foreign capital inflow to fund the excessive domestic spending. Indeed, massive foreign funds flowed into the region, helping to create asset bubbles in the regional economies by pushing up asset prices way above the levels justified by fundamental factors. But investors totally ignored this dangerous current account deficit signal in the years before the Asian crisis due to their blind confidence in Asia's ability to deliver sufficient income growth to pay off foreign investors and creditors.

The region suffered a significant setback in foreign trade in 1996 and 1997, as the US dollar soared through the roof. As Asia's exchange rates were fixed against the US dollar at that time, the rising US dollar also pushed up Asian currencies sharply. This badly hurt Asia's export competitiveness. The negative impact of this exchange rate shock on Asia's economies was significant due to the region's heavy reliance on exports for

---

[1] This is a broader concept of external imbalance than a trade deficit. The current account includes services trade and income transfers in addition to merchandise trade that is included in the trade account.

economic growth. The shock thus acted as a wake-up call for those investors' unrealistic expectations on Asia's income and corporate earnings growth.

All of a sudden, investor concern about Asia's large current account deficits (which averaged over 5% of the total size of the economy) returned. This shook their confidence in Asia's ability to meet its external payments and earnings expectations, thus darkening the outlook for the region's stock markets. As investors started selling down Asian stocks, the asset bubble burst. Massive outflow of hot money became detrimental when investors fled the region and speculators exploited free capital mobility to attack the Asian currency regimes by borrowing Asian currencies to sell – a speculative action called short-selling.

However, none of the conventional currency crisis theories could provide a complete account for the outbreak of the Asian crisis because none of the key elements of these theories were present prior to the crisis. The essence of the currency crisis theories is about market expectations of the sustainability of a fixed exchange rate regime under different sets of economic environments. There are two major variants for the currency crisis theory. They both focus on government economic management policies, including its funding and debt payment ability and policy credibility to keep investor confidence.

One variant centres on the problem of persistent government fiscal deficit within a fixed exchange rate regime. The crux of this argument lies in the financing of the government budget deficit by printing money. If the government prints money to finance the prolonged fiscal deficit, and at the same time uses its limited stock of foreign exchange reserves to sustain the fixed exchange rate, it would be brewing a financial disaster of its own making. This is because printing money would increase the supply of the currency in the market, thus putting downward pressure on its exchange rate. If the government continues printing money, the supply pressure of the local currency on the foreign exchange market will mount and eventually make the fixed exchange rate unsustainable. In other words, the exchange rate will crack under the mountain of supply pressure, as the limited stock of foreign reserves will be too small to sustain it.

More crucially, financing the fiscal deficit by printing money would create excessive demand and instil investor nervousness about the surging inflation. Soaring inflation would then create an enlarging current account deficit by boosting domestic costs and eroding export competitiveness, while sucking in imports to satisfy domestic demand. Since a rising current account deficit means more capital outflow (for import payments) than inflow (from export receipts), it exerts massive downward pressure on the exchange rate. Thus, investors would anticipate an eventual currency collapse as a result of the deteriorating current account deficit. This currency devaluation is a necessary step to correct the current account deficit, as the currency fall helps to boost exports (by making them cheaper) and reduce imports (by making them dearer). Just this expectation *per se* would be enough to generate speculative attack on the currency in question, disregarding whether surging inflation has actually emerged. Once confidence has collapsed, any attempts to defend the fixed exchange rate would drain the government's foreign reserves and ultimately lead to a currency crisis.

The other variant focuses on a government's policy credibility under a fixed exchange rate regime. At times, a government faces the policy dilemma of whether to defend its fixed exchange rate by making a trade off between short-term economic gains, such as boosting economic and employment growth, and long-term management credibility that delivers economic stability. If it is seen as pursuing myopic policies to maximise short-term gains at the expense of long-term stability, investors will expect major economic problems to emerge when the short-term gains manifest into an economic bubble, worsening fiscal balances, rising inflation, and the like. Such expectations will shake investor confidence and generate panic and speculative attack on the currency.

Once confidence is lost, investors and speculators will expect the government's poor policy management to damage the economic system and its investment environment. They will start pulling out of the economy and sell the currency, betting that any official attempt to defend the fixed exchange rate would fail due to policy errors and an expected economic breakdown. A downward spiral on the currency in question could develop as a result of a self-fulfilling prophecy of repeated currency sales by market players. As players sell the currency, they drive down the exchange rate. A falling currency, in turn, acts to justify the market expectation of poor economic management and further currency losses, prompting more players to sell. The downward spiral will eventually lead to a currency collapse, taking the economy with it.

However, prior to the regional crisis, there was no evidence that Asian economies had experienced the economic woes described by these conventional currency crisis theories. In particular, the regional governments did not suffer from persistent fiscal deficits prior to the regional debacle. So there was no need for them to print money to finance their fiscal books. Nor were they engaged in a runaway money printing process to boost economic growth. There was also no evidence of rampant inflation in the pre-crisis years. Though Asian inflation rates were higher than that in the US, against whose currency Asia was pegged before the crisis, they were not excessively high.

What about economic growth? Fast deteriorating economic conditions could have tempted Asian governments to forgo their fixed exchange rate systems to regain monetary flexibility to boost domestic growth. Why? Under a fixed exchange rate system, the government loses its monetary policy flexibility because it can only adjust money supply to protect the fixed exchange rate but nothing else. In other words, when there is selling pressure on the local currency, the authorities will reduce money supply to shore up the exchange rate. Conversely, when there is upward pressure, they will increase money supply to curb the currency's appreciating pressure. All these monetary policy moves are implemented to keep the exchange rate fixed at the official rate independent of any other economic needs, such as economic growth.

So, when economic conditions worsen, the government may want to increase money supply to boost growth. But doing so would put downward pressure on the exchange rate, threatening to destroy the fixed exchange rate regime. Therefore, mounting economic pains, like a deepening economic recession and surging unemployment, could prompt Asian governments to abandon their fixed exchange rate policy to regain the freedom of using monetary policy to boost growth. However, economic conditions in Asia were not dire before the crisis, although there was a slowdown in growth in 1996. Unemployment rates across Asia remained benign when the crisis broke. Thus, there was no compelling reason to believe that regional governments had intended to pursue massive monetary expansion to boost growth at the expense of their fixed exchange rate regimes.

The Financial Culprit

Crucially, the conventional currency crisis theories have missed two significant aspects – asset market bubble and financial distortion – that were prevailing in the Asian economies before the regional crisis. There was a boom-bust cycle across the region's asset markets, where stock and land prices soared first and then plunged. And these asset market bubbles were closely related to the financial distortion in their systems. Thus, if there is one single most important factor contributing to the Asian crisis, it is the weakness in the region's financial systems. Insufficient capital adequacy ratios, poor regulations on bank lending, opaque and loose asset classification systems, poor loan-loss provisioning, and lack of transparency of banks were common traits of most Asian banking systems.

In all of the crisis-hit countries, notably South Korea, Indonesia and Thailand, the financial systems were politicised. Capital allocation, like bank lending, was based on political decision and choice without reference to commercial criteria and risk assessment. Vested interests and greed also unduly affected financial decisions at banks, giving rise to corruption. Worse still, these politicised systems created a wrong impression to investors that governments would guarantee risky investments, thus eliminating prudent management and decisions. This perceived government guarantee encouraged many investors, especially the politically connected ones, to blindly pour money into bad investments at the expense of other sensible but politically unconnected projects. In economics, this problem of selfishness hurting public interest is called the moral hazard problem (see next section).

For example, it was widely known that South Korea had an

explicit too-big-to-fail policy for her banks due to the government's close relationship with the financial system. Indeed, in October 1997, when the Asian crisis spread to Northeast Asia from the south, the South Korean government decided to nationalise bad and unviable banks instead of closing them. Similar practices were also seen in most Southeast Asian economies, such as the "TIM" economies, before the crisis. Politicised banking systems in Asia are indeed an area in which crony capitalism might have played a significant role in brewing the regional financial crisis.

Under these politicised systems, financial liberalisation across Asia had backfired and exacerbated the structural fault line in the financial systems. During the early 1990s, Southeast Asian economies were caught up in a global wave of financial liberalisation. Laws barring capital flows were scrapped. Tax incentives also encouraged offshore borrowing by local financial intermediaries. A notable example was Thailand's banks and non-bank financial intermediaries, which borrowed excessively via the offshore Bangkok International Banking Facilities (BIBF) before the crisis. The borrowed foreign funds were put back into the local economy, feeding excessive investments until the asset bubble burst after the collapse of the Thai baht in July 1997.

However, the deregulation was not done properly. The development of regulatory rules and agencies lagged far behind the pressing need of supervision of financial institutions. This had led to bad management, poor accounting, fraud, and imprudent lending. Asian banks' poor regulatory infrastructure was characterised by politicised lending, poor enforcement of existing regulations, and the lack of a safety net to prevent systemic failures. Government-directed lending was found most strongly in Indonesia, South Korea, Malaysia, Philippines, and Thailand. Loans to connected firms were also a very crucial part of the banking business, especially in Indonesia, Malaysia, and South Korea. All the crisis-hit economies had weak regulatory controls and poor accounting standards, which worsened the problem of heavy political intervention in lending decisions. With the exception of the Philippines, the crisis-hit economies also had little safety net, in terms of deposit insurance, to contain the potential risks of bank runs that could erupt in their systems.

This poor regulatory infrastructure had fermented the banking crises in regional economies. All it needed was a trigger to pull them off. And the trigger was put in place by the influx of hot money.

A change in the composition of capital flows into Asia in the 1990s had further deepened the region's financial flaws, intensifying its financial stress that finally set off the financial crisis. While much of capital inflows in the 1980s were in the form of foreign direct investment, the composition shifted to more liquid portfolio investment in the 1990s. This portfolio inflow not only funded Asia's widening current account deficit, but also fueled its asset bubble in the first half of the 1990s. For example, much of Asia's investment was concentrated on land and property before the regional crisis. When the crisis hit, most of those good old property loans turned bad, piling into bad loans that defaulted either on interest or principal payments or both.

The crisis-infected economies in Asia had three quarters or more of their collateral assets tied up in real estate in 1997. Among them, South Korea, Indonesia, Malaysia, and Thailand had the highest proportion, with collateral valuation amounting to 90% of their assets. After the regional crisis broke and the asset bubble burst, many of these property loans turned bad. The percentage of loans that defaulted on interest payments for at least three months, or the so-called non-performing loans (or bad loans), jumped sharply from an average of 8.4% of total loan assets to 14% within a year after the crisis broke. The three crisis-hit economies of South Korea, Indonesia, and Thailand all recorded 20% or more non-performing loans, while Malaysia, Thailand, and Hong Kong saw their bad debts jump by more than two-fold between 1997 and 1998. But this may not be all because the regional banks' data may have underestimated the true amount of bad debts due to Asia's dodgy definition of a non-performing loan. While the international community defines non-performing loans as those that have unpaid interest for three months, most Asian economies had much looser definitions, such as six months or even one year. Hence, some private sector analysts' estimates had put many Asian economies' bad debt ratios at double the amount of the official reported numbers.

Local banks and non-bank financial institutions funded the excessive investment with a general perception that the governments would guarantee the big companies and projects. Using the same land, or property, and financial assets as collateral, most Asian financial institutions lent repeatedly to different speculators for further punting in the property and stock markets. This created a self-feeding upward spiral on lending and asset prices. As they lent to fund asset purchases, the speculative buying pushed up the value of the existing collateral, thereby inflating the lending institutions' capital base and allowing them to lend more, which in turn drove asset prices higher.

Also fostering Asia's asset bubble was increased competition, resulting from financial deregulation, between local banks and non-bank financial institutions. Keen competition had led to sharp erosion of profit margins, prompting many banks to lend to risky businesses in the late 1980s and early 1990s in the hope of boosting their returns. As this process evolved, the composition of foreign capital inflow began to change, with portfolio investment and short-term bank lending accounting for an increasing share of capital inflow. In South Korea and the ASEAN4 countries (Philippines, Malaysia, Indonesia, and Thailand), net portfolio capital inflow jumped from almost nothing in 1990 to 4% of their average GDP just prior to the crisis. On the other hand, the share of other types of longer-term capital inflow, like long-term bank loans and foreign direct investment, remained relatively stagnant.

Local banks welcomed the influx of this hot money as they were looking for cheaper ways to secure funding under intense competition. Thus, they borrowed heavily from foreign lenders, often as short-term loans, and used the money to fund long-term local projects. This created a serious so-called balance sheet mismatch problem, which was the final nail to the coffin of Asia's broken financial system. When local banks borrowed short-term loans from overseas lenders, these loans were denominated in foreign currencies. They were then converted into the local currencies and invested in long-term projects. These borrowing arrangements created two mismatching problems in the local banks' balance sheets. One is currency mismatching and the other is loan-maturity mismatching.

Currency mismatching exposed banks to foreign exchange risk – as and when the local currency dropped sharply, the debt burden of the foreign currency loan soared. This is because more local currency was needed to exchange a given amount of foreign currency to repay the loan. Loan-maturity mismatching exposed the banks to interest rate risk – as and when interest rates surged, the banks' funding cost also surged as they borrowed short-term and thus needed to renew the loans frequently at the prevailing (rising) interest rates. But their return from the long-term investment was fixed. Thus, soaring funding cost under fixed income pushed banks into financial difficulties.

While there were various financial vehicles that banks could use to offset, or hedge, their foreign exchange risk, they did not do so believing that their governments would sustain the fixed exchange rate regimes forever. Thus, the resultant build-up of external liabilities was in the form of unhedged debts, giving rise to significant currency risk in the banking systems. The naive belief that Asian governments would keep their fixed exchange rate systems had also eliminated any perceivable currency risk for foreign creditors. Together with higher Asian interest rates relative to other countries, the fixed exchange rate regimes thus enticed massive foreign lending, often imprudently, to Asia.

Reliance on liquid hot money inflows had left Asia's domestic financial system susceptible to foreign interest rate hikes and/or domestic currency depreciation. The balance sheet mismatch problems inherent in the region's banking system only exacerbated these problems. When a surging US dollar hit Asia by destroying its export competitiveness in 1996 and 1997, investor confidence crumbled. Foreign creditors and many local investors withdrew *en masse* from the region, unwinding the upward spiral process that built the asset bubble. Local interest rates soared to prevent capital outflow. But instead of curbing capital flight, they only crashed the regional economic systems.

Asset prices began to fall on soaring interest rates and capital outflow, creating bad loans and eroding the value of collateral. Lending contracted, reducing asset prices further, creating more bad loans and destroying more collateral. The upward spiral process that fueled Asia's asset bubbles quickly reversed itself into a downward spiral and pierced the bubbles. Foreign lending also dried up. And as stock markets fell, more capital fled Asia when both local and foreign investors rushed for exit. Such a rush, in turn, created a massive selling pressure on Asian currencies, draining the region's official foreign exchange reserves, crashing the currency regimes and ending in economic collapse.

Moral Hazard

What all this suggests is that the Asian crisis was indeed the bursting of a regional financial bubble, with the currency crises in the individual economies more a symptom than a cause of this debacle. The problem began with the financial intermediaries, whose liabilities were incorrectly seen as having an implicit government guarantee. But these financial institutions were in fact poorly regulated and thus subject to the so-called moral hazard problem.

In the financial sector, the moral hazard problem arises when poor regulations encourage or tempt financial institutions to pursue their self-interest and maximise profit via imprudent lending and investment and corruption at the expense of public interest. Their selfish behaviour often sabotages the functioning of the whole financial system. This was what happened to Asia prior to the crisis. Excessive risky lending was fostered by loose regulations and inflow of portfolio capital, creating a regional asset bubble characterised by soaring property and stock prices.

Asia's experience shows that moral hazard also arose from the depositor side. The perception of governments guaranteeing their banks removed depositors' incentive to monitor the depository institutions' behaviour, thus imposing no discipline on these institutions' lending and investment policies. Prior to the Asian crisis, Asian depositors had too much confidence in their banks because they thought their governments would not allow their banks to fail. Hence, they put money blindly into those financial institutions that offered the highest interest rate without asking why. Any rational depositor should know that higher risk is associated with high interest rates offered. But obviously, this simple rule of prudence was thrown out of the window during the bubble years. The depositors' moral hazard helped fuel Asia's asset bubbles since they supplied imprudent banks with ample funding for speculative investment.

Thus, overvalued Asian assets were sustained by some sort of a spiral process, in which massive bank lending drove up the price of risky assets and made the balance sheets of financial intermediaries look stronger than they were. Then, the external shock of a soaring US dollar crashed Asia's export competitiveness and refocused investors' attention on the region's unsustainable huge current account deficits and foreign liabilities. When investors woke up from unrealistic profit growth expectations, their confidence was shattered and the resultant massive withdrawal from Asia eventually led to a tearful ending of Asia's party in 1997.

The problem of moral hazard played an important role in deepening Asia's financial flaws. Asian governments' intervention in and connection with the local financial systems was seen, in many cases, as implicit or even explicit government guarantee of private sector liabilities. The situation was similar to the US savings and loan debacle in the 1980s. When the US Federal Savings & Loan Insurance Corporation guaranteed savings in the thrift institutions, US depositors had no incentive to monitor the lendings from these institutions, which were basically money out of their deposit accounts. The lack of market discipline thus encouraged these institutions to pursue risky businesses. On the other hand, the thrift management had little incentive to follow prudent business practices because they were investing (or betting in some sense) with their clients' money that was insured by the US government. Thus, government guarantee created a moral hazard problem among both the depositors and the thrifts.

In Asia, regional governments practised *de facto* guarantee policies for financial (and in many cases large non-financial) institutions because of their belief that these institutions were "too big to fail", and because politicians had vested interests in the financial system. Especially notable were Thai finance companies and South Korean banks before the crisis, whose funds were blindly believed by depositors to have been underwritten completely by the government. Thus, like the fixed exchange rate regimes eliminating currency risk for foreign investors in Asia, these government guarantees helped eliminate investment risk for both local and foreign investors. This resulted in a rampant moral hazard problem and made Asian banking business grow like it was risk-free. The growth hype was like flipping a coin with heads the banks win, tails the government (hence taxpayer) loses. But the taxpayer was blindfolded by the government's too-big-to-fail policy. Thus, Asia's financial sector grew excessively even though it was against the public interest of sound business practices and prudent management.

Self-Fulfilling Pessimism

To a large extent, the huge financial excess in Asia was fueled by international speculation that drove Asian asset values to unrealistic levels, and by an Asian variant of crony capitalism that drove investment to unproductive ends. These investment excesses created a boom-bust cycle across the region's asset markets before 1997. This sequence of events suggests that the financial crisis was the real driver behind the regional debacle, with the series of currency crises in 1997 and 1998 in the individual economies merely a symptom of the process but not a cause.

The ability of the crisis to spread to economies that did not have strong economic and systemic linkages suggests that there must be something intangible that caused a financial contagion. Such an intangible factor was likely a self-fulfilling financial panic. Pre-crisis evidence shows that the macroeconomic conditions of some of the Asian economies, notably those in Northeast Asia, were not weak enough to sink their systems. Direct economic and financial links between Northeast, except Japan, and Southeast Asia were also not strong. But the speed and magnitude of the crisis that swept through Asia suggested that there must have been other ways for the domino effect to spread. Financial panic among local and foreign investors, who yanked their funds out of the region in a short period of time, played an important role in delivering a sweeping contagion effect. This panic, in turn, created a downward spiral of falling asset prices and financial failures that rendered the regional system dysfunctional.

The financial panic was an internal force generated within

Asia. This force stemmed from an indirect linkage between the regional economies through competition in third country markets. For example, a significant currency devaluation by Thailand put a large negative pressure on other Asian exporting economies since they export similar products to third markets, notably the US, Europe, and Japan. However, such indirect linkages through export competitive pressure was not the only force to cause a regional crisis with the magnitude as seen in 1997 and 1998. There was another force originating from outside the Asian system that aggravated this third-market-linkage effect and pushed Asia over the cliff.

This culprit was likely to be herd instinct. This herd theory stems from the fact that investors' ability to manage their portfolios decreases as global investment opportunities increase. When international investors are facing an expanded and fragmented investment horizon, time and resources constraints will prevent them from studying all individual markets in great detail and due diligence. Thus, investors' direct knowledge of local market conditions decreases as global investment opportunities rise. They have to rely more on their observations of the actions of other investors, who may have better or even insider information of local conditions, rather than on their analysis of local developments. So, once a major investor, who is seen as having better information, moves in a particular direction, the whole crowd of other fund managers follows. Since stakeholders judge the performance of many large investors, like pension funds, by their investment returns relative to other managers or markets, these investors have a strong tendency to follow the herd to minimise the risk of under-performing their peers.

Another related herd contagion is the "birds of the same feather flock together" mentality, as investors with imperfect information tend to treat certain economies as one group. In Asia's case, Northeast and Southeast Asian economies were treated as one collective group of Asian economies. Hence, events in one member economy were attributed to all members in the whole group. When an economic shock occurred in one of the economies, it was transmitted throughout the group disregarding the individual members' economic and financial differences. Both forms of herd mentality were well observed during the Asian crisis.

In a nutshell, the Asian crisis differs from other previous developing world crises in several key aspects. First, it was a confidence crisis, which manifested into rampant capital outflow, that pulled down the whole financial system. It was more than a current account crisis – brought about by significant import-export imbalance – as seen in most emerging markets. Second, unlike other confidence crises in the 1980s and the early 1990s, its root causes were structural – premature liberalisation of financial markets without adequate supervision and regulation, crony capitalism, and policy mistakes in managing private capital flows – and not weak macroeconomic fundamentals. The Asian crisis involved private-to-private capital flows, not fiscal profligacy or excessive monetary expansion. Third, it was not a solvency crisis, like those in Latin America where governments went bankrupt. Asian governments were not broke. If there were no massive capital flight, the Asian economies might not have sunk. The Asian crisis was a liquidity crisis.

If governments fail to manage their economies prudently, this new type of crisis will likely occur with greater frequency in the developing world, including Asia, as globalisation and market integration intensify. Many recent crises, including the Asian and Mexican crises, were in fact twin crisis – banking as well as currency crises. The economic cost of a twin crisis is much higher than a pure banking or currency crisis. In nominal terms, the Asian Development Bank estimates that a twin crisis would cost as much as 20% of gross domestic product (GDP) in lost output, compared to about half of this amount from a single crisis.

In terms of recovery time, the cost has also risen sharply. Evidence shows that the average recovery time from a twin crisis is about 2.6 years, compared to 1.5 years for a pure currency crisis and 1.9 years for a pure banking crisis. Developing economies have limited experience with institutional and prudential safeguards for containing the risks of globalisation. Thus, twin financial crises can be expected to occur with increasing frequency and rising costs to the economy, as globalisation and reforms in the developing world, including Asia, continue.

With increasing economic integration becoming a fact of life, structural reforms are the only way to minimise the risk of a financial crisis. During and after the Asian crisis, there was no lack of research to advise regional authorities on getting their economies back on track to sustainable growth. Structural reforms and better regulatory controls were the core policy prescriptions. Besides, regional authorities were supposed to formulate macroeconomic policies to stabilise the exchange rate, to nurture a suitable liquidity environment for overhauling the financial system and the corporate sector, and to prevent a similar crisis from happening again.

If the macro and structural policy mix were right, it should regain investor confidence and attract foreign capital inflow to Asia again. Tough structural reforms would purge the regional economic excess and put Asia's savings and investment back in balance. The road to efficiency would have looked bright had the regional governments kept up with their reform efforts. While there was a strong start to reform in the year after the crisis, notably by South Korea and Thailand who were dubbed at one point as model reform pupils under the IMF economic assistance programmes, Asia slipped on reform subsequently. There was a certain amount of financial and corporate restructuring done after the crisis, but they were inadequate in view of the inefficiencies in the system that needed to be purged.

Evidence also shows that Asia had cheated in many ways to avoid the badly needed but painful structural changes (see the next chapter). This denial will lead to a prolonged and painful period of correction in the coming years, as Asia enters a new economic paradigm with China emitting competitive stress and global excess demand not emerging to salvage Asia, as it did in the 1980s and 1990s.

Chapter 2

Asia Cheats on Reforms

One would expect Asia to have learnt from the painful experience of the 1997/1998 regional financial crisis, and picked up the pieces left behind by the disaster by purging financial excesses and fixing the economic woes. In particular, the region needs to implement painful structural reforms to strengthen its banking and corporate sectors. These changes include not only recapitalising the banks, but also uprooting the banks' policy lending role, cutting bad debts, reducing moral hazard, and increasing market discipline for monitoring lending practices, improving bank and corporate transparency, accountability and management, and purging cronyism. The corporates also need to cut their huge debt burden, change their short-sighted, quick-profit trading practice, and focus on long-term profitability and efficiency. Asia as a whole needs to shift from the low-efficiency, manufacturing-based export-oriented economic model to a high value-added, service-based, consumption-oriented model.

However, despite strong economic recovery in 1999 and 2000, which should have provided favourable macro conditions for implementing economic reforms, the regional governments have not grasped the opportunity to restructure their economies thoroughly. Thus, many of the structural woes still remain. This means that the old economic excesses were not completely eliminated. But a new over-investment cycle has developed during the robust output rebound after the Asian crisis. These old excesses and the inherent structural flaws have remained a major drag on the region's growth momentum because they impair the regional banking system and hamper the revival of domestic demand.

That is why, with the benefit of hindsight, Asia's post-crisis economic recovery lasted for only about two-and-a-half years under this mountain of excess capacity. In addition, punctured asset market bubbles and curbed domestic demand by broken banking systems are major reasons why Asia is stuck with falling prices and wealth erosion even five years after the regional debacle. Some Asian economies, clinging to an export-led growth model that had served them well, have compounded the problem by refusing to cut output to boost prices. The global economic slowdown, led by the US in 2001, was only an excuse for Asia's short-lived economic recovery. The real culprit for restraining the region's growth ability and domestic demand potential was insufficient reform.

Excess capacity is not just an Asian phenomenon. It is a global problem with investment bubbles, especially in the high-tech and information technology sectors, developed in the mid-1990s in major economies such as the US and Europe. Given the significant amount of over-investment, excess capacity will continue to plague the world economy for years. But global demand will remain constrained in the coming years due to the build-up of a formidable debt burden in the global economy resulted from over-spending by the private sector in the major economies (see Chapters 3 and 8).

Under these circumstances, the intense pressure from goods suppliers to sell into markets with feeble demand will manifest itself in weak pricing power, corporate profit squeezing, and constrained economic growth. All this, in turn, will create long-term downward pressure on many Asian asset prices and currencies throughout this decade. In other words, long gone are the good old days of fast growth and easy money from surging asset prices.

Acknowledging the Changes

Nevertheless, economic improvement and some reform achievements in Asia must be acknowledged. Asian economies rebounded sharply after the regional crisis. Notably, the crisis-hit countries of South Korea, Indonesia, and Thailand enjoyed sharp and swift economic recovery, with their economic growth rebounding like a "V" shape – plunging in 1998 but only to surge back in the following year. In South Korea, output fell by 7% in 1998, but over the next 12 months, it surged by 11%. In Thailand, GDP dropped by over 10% in the first year, only to rebound by 4% the next. Even in Indonesia, the worst hit economy by the crisis, GDP plunged by 13% in 1998 but snapped back to 1% growth in 1999. Just as the region had been applauded too euphorically in the years leading up to the crisis, so too was the mood of gloom overdone in the immediate aftermath.

Meanwhile, the region's external credit positions had improved sharply. Foreign liabilities, as approximated by international bank loans to Asia, had been cut by over 40% since late 1997. According to the Bank for International Settlements, which is the central bank for the world's central banks, total international bank loans to Asia dropped steadily from US$70 billion in 1997 to US$40 billion in 2001. Asia's current account balances of foreign goods and services trade had also turned around sharply. National statistics show that they were in deep deficit positions of over 5% of GDP before and during the crisis, but had reversed to surpluses averaging 8.6% of GDP after the 1997/1998 crisis.

Improvement is also seen at the country level. The most noticeable example is South Korea, which received US$58 billion in bailout funds from the International Monetary Fund (IMF) in late 1997 in exchange for financial reforms. Many South Koreans resented the IMF assistance programme, as it demanded changes that rocked the old system, hurt vested interests, and inflicted economic pains that created massive unemployment. Nevertheless, for all their resentment, South Korea still embraced and implemented the IMF's reforms. This contrasts sharply with Japan's reform denial throughout the 1990s. Seoul's reform resolve was strong, at least at the beginning. It stepped in to recapitalise the banks by injecting 156 trillion won (US$130 billion) into the system. It was also the first Asian government to set up a public asset management company after the Asian crisis to buy up bad loans from the banks. The effort paid off well for South Korea, as Seoul had retired its bailout-related debts ahead of schedule.

More crucially, the recapitalisation programme had freed South Korean banks to get on with business. With fresh capital and healthier loan portfolios, South Korean banks were able to lend again soon after the Asian crisis. This rapid resumption of bank lending was not seen in other Asian economies, except China where bank loans were still policy driven. Just as crucially, South Korean banks had also overhauled their lending practices. They became more responsive to competitive pressure. Despite the failures of several merger and acquisition deals, private investors and some foreign financial institutions had nevertheless bought, and thus injected foreign management and discipline into a number of small South Korean banks. The independents had also consolidated, cut costs, and boosted their market scope. The post-crisis South Korean banking environment has focused on consumer lending, which now accounts for about half of bank loan assets, compared to almost nil before the Asian crisis.

Seoul also helped by refraining somewhat from meddling with the banks (but political intervention still remains a problem; see below) after recapitalising the banks. It laid down new lending guidelines, including setting up of independent credit committees, for banks to manage credit risks. It also required conglomerates to cut debt, sell off non-core businesses, and, in some cases, close down altogether. All this has broadened the banks' lending scope, making room for small and medium businesses to borrow.

South Korea's strong start in banking reform created a robust growth momentum within the domestic sector that was not seen in other Asian neighbours. Booming domestic demand thus helped cushion the economy from the global economic slowdown in 2001 and 2002 and gave its workforce and consumers strong confidence that was absent in other regional economies, except China. The political will, with the assistance of the IMF discipline, was crucial as it was Seoul's effort to reform the financial system that triggered the changes in the economy, not the other way round.

In Southeast Asia, some structural changes have also taken

place, notably in Thailand. For example, Siam City Cement Public Company Ltd. used to be a company that displayed all classical Thai syndromes. It was bureaucratic, hierarchical, conservative, and inefficient. Its staff spent most of their time in politicking, petty fights, mundane work, and paper shuffling. A western-style focus on profits and accountability was totally unknown to Siam. But the Asian crisis, which had its origins in Thailand, changed all that. At the time of the crisis, Siam City was debt-strapped with a heavy US$720 million burden that it could not service. The founding Ratanarak family was finally forced to sell 25% of the company to the Swiss cement giant, Holderbank Financiere Glaris Ltd. (now Holcim Ltd.). It also gave the Swiss management control. Three years after the Asian crisis, Siam City emerged from its woes as a lean, focused, and productive company. Another example is the Bangkok-based melamine and plastic tableware firm Srithai Superware. It turned a profit in 2001 for the first time since the 1997 regional crisis. It has restructured its US$173 million foreign debt and is upgrading its operations and increasing exports. Many other Thai companies did similar deals to relieve themselves of debt burdens when the Thai baht slumped in 1997.

Overall, there are also signs of progress in banking reform. The few banks, notably those in South Korea which has closed or merged over 600 financial institutions, that have vigorously revamped their loan procedures and created effective and autonomous loan workout units have shown successful recovery. Almost all Asian governments have set up asset management companies to take over bad loans from banks. According to estimates by management consultants, McKinsey Co. Ltd., by mid-2002, Asia's asset management companies have acquired a total of about US$350 billion of bad debt from banks and recovered about 30% of these bad loans via asset sales and debt restructuring programmes.

The initial signs of successful economic and structural changes had led to improvement in foreign sentiment. At least for a short while, foreigners became eager to lend to and invest in Asia again. Foreign money poured back into Asia between 1999 and 2001, reducing the borrowing cost for many Asian corporates. As a result, Asia's risk premium plunged during these three years. This premium is measured by the higher interest rate that Asian borrowers have to pay over and above the rate that the most creditworthy international borrowers pay. For example, during the peak of the Asian crisis, an average Indonesian borrower had to pay over four percentage points more in interest rate than a good-credit international borrower in getting a loan. But this interest rate differential fell to about half a percentage point after the crisis. Other Asian borrowers experienced the same positive changes in their borrowing environment.

Illusive Healing

However, the plunge in Asia's risk premium after the regional crisis was ironic. This is because there remained serious structural problems in Asia despite its reform efforts. In other words, the sharp drop in the risk premium was not justified. Foreign investors should have asked for higher interest rates when they lent to Asia after the crisis to compensate for the region's inherent high credit risk. But the fact that they did not do so reflected many investors' overly optimistic assumption about Asia's ability to deliver satisfactory reform progress to rationalise their now-proven misjudged investment decision in the region.

Looking deeper, Asia's economic healing process has, to a fair extent, been illusive, as economic restructuring has never been sufficient. The "V" shape output rebound between 1999 and early 2001 had masked the urgency for structural reforms in many Asian countries. The strong headline economic growth acted as a force to weaken reform resolve. Another major problem with Asia's reforms is that they are piecemeal. Anecdotal evidence for structural changes does not add up to the macroeconomic trends. This suggests that despite the noticeable reform efforts by some Asian economies, overall changes had been insufficient relative to the amount of economic inefficiency in the system.

While optimists like to generalise the success stories of the South Korean banks' retrenchment and Siam City's and Srithai Superware's transformation, their anecdotes are not robust. For every transformed South Korean bank and Thai company, there are many more financial and non-financial institutions in Asia that refuse to cut their debts, that balk at restructuring, and continue to stick with their old inefficient habits. Of the three economies that received IMF bailouts during the crisis, only South Korea has used the crisis to effect some structural changes, but they are still insufficient (see below). Thailand and South Korea have also back-peddled on reform programmes after a strong start in 1998. Indonesia still seems to be wondering what hit it back in 1997! Hence, the painful effects of corporate and bank retrenchment will remain a drag on economic growth for many years.

Many Asian corporates have been cheating on their restructuring efforts with little or no incentive to cut domestic debt (even the South Koreans are not spared the scrutiny). Aggregate domestic debt data shows the problem clearly. Despite its sharp cut in external debt, Asia's domestic debt as a percentage of GDP fell by only 14% in 1999 from the beginning of the Asian financial crisis. This was hardly a sufficient reduction compared to Asia's pressing need to reduce the debt burden to free up resources for both economic growth and reform. Domestic debt in China, South Korea, and Thailand actually rose steadily after the regional crisis. Overall, Southeast Asian economies have a much bigger domestic and foreign debt burden than Northeast Asia.

The lack of domestic debt reduction in fact reveals the flaws of Asia's timid economic restructuring, which has relied mainly on equity issuance as the main way to improve balance sheet liquidity of companies. Indeed, Asian equity-financing activity – by selling stocks and equity rights and warrants through the equity market to source funding – jumped by over 50% between 1998 and 1999. This indicates that Asian companies were aggressively tapping the stock market to raise funds, while doing little to pare down their huge domestic debt load after the regional crisis. Such behaviour was in fact cheating on the painful restructuring needs. To see this, consider the common measure of corporate health: the debt-to-equity ratio.

The logic is that if the debt-to-equity ratio of a company rises, it shows a rising debt burden on the company relative to its equity asset. This rising burden in turn drains the company's resources by channeling them away from productive investment towards servicing debts. Hence, a high and/or rising debt-to-equity ratio (normally 25% or more for a manufacturing company) is bad for corporate health, but a low and/or declining ratio is good. Now put this logic into Asia's post-crisis perspective. Since Asia did little to cut debt, the numerator of the ratio remained more or less constant. But the surge in equity issuance inflated the denominator of the ratio. Hence, the region's debt-to-equity ratio dropped, as reported widely by the media after the crisis. But this produced a false sense of improvement in corporate Asia's financial health because the drop was due to equity issuance, not debt reduction. Even if we take the drop with a leap of faith, most Asian corporate debt-to-equity ratios still remain above 100%. In other words, the excessive debt burden on Asia's corporate balance sheets remains a problem.

Take the favourite reform model, South Korea, for example. The average debt-to-equity ratio for corporate South Korea fell to about 150% in 2000 from 500% in 1997 (and it still remains above 100% today). Productivity and average return-on-equity were higher, especially for companies in the burgeoning services sector. However, there was not much improvement in real profitability. Local corporate surveys in early 2002 found that only a third of South Korea's 144 largest public companies were expected to make profits exceeding their cost of capital in the year, and only 21 of the total made back their capital costs in 2000. This lack of improvement in profits is not surprising because the drastic drop in corporate South Korea's debt-to-equity ratio was a deceiving result of massive equity and rights issuance by South Korean corporations after the Asian crisis instead of much needed debt reduction.

The IMF echoed this concern when its Director Stanley Fisher noted in a speech in Seoul in late 2001 that South Korea's corporate sector remained heavily indebted by international standards and thus suffered from poor profitability. He also raised the concern that large distressed South Korean firms still had the capacity to destabilise financial markets and drag the economy. Meanwhile, South Korea's own data also illustrate a setback in reform efforts. The official Financial Supervisory Service reported in July 2001 that debt-to-equity ratios of South Korean companies had crept back up after an initial decline. Hyundai was the worst performer, with a ratio of 478%. *De ja vu!*

Corporate Asia's avoidance of debt reduction ran into problems after mid-2001, when equity prices plunged on the bursting of the high-tech investment bubble. The market crash made the issue of new company stocks more difficult. Increased risk aversion among foreign investors towards Asian markets after the burst of the global asset bubble had prompted them to withdraw again from the region, thus aggravating Asia's market difficulty. The cost of capital in many Asian economies, notably again in South Korea, remains very high. This reflects that investors and creditors had remained wary of the region. Thus, they have asked for higher lending interest rates or dividend yields for investing in Asia. South Korea has also experienced extreme difficulties in selling off corporate assets, such as Seoul Bank, Daewoo Motor, Hynix, and three financial affiliates of the Hyundai Group, to foreign investors, despite great strides made by the government in improving the macro economy. This experience shows that structural reforms to fix balance sheet problems and improve corporate governance were crucial to regain investor confidence and secure long-term growth.

But Asia has missed the opportunity to do so. The stubbornly high bad debt level across the region, except Hong Kong and Singapore, is another piece of evidence of Asia's lack of serious reforms. In Asia, loans with unpaid interest of over three months, or non-performing loans, rose 33% to US$2 trillion in 2000 and 2001, despite a concerted effort by officials to bring the nagging problem under control. The deterioration of global economic conditions in these two years was only part of the reason for the rise in bad loans. Complacency in financial reform and an incentive to hide banking problems were also culprits.

The private sector's estimate of 33% rise in non-performing loans was roughly double the official increase reported by the regional authorities. From the official government perspective, while this private estimate is controversial, the discrepancy stems from the difference between the treatment of non-performing loans by the private and public sectors. The private sector has a more stringent definition for bad loans. It includes those that had been moved off bank balance sheets by many national authorities to asset management companies. These asset management companies were set up to help recapitalise the regional banking sectors by buying bad loans from banks and re-selling them in the market to recoup some of the losses. Thus, government officials exclude these loans in the asset management companies from the bad loan classification on the blind assumption that they could be sold off without any problems.

However, the general inability of asset management companies to sell off the bad assets they acquired has made them predominantly bad debt warehouses. In other words, merely moving non-performing loans from bank balance sheets to asset management companies does not solve the problem. Selling or resolving bad loans and returning the assets to the private sector is the ultimate solution. Classifying all problem loans in the asset management companies as permanent bad loan assets may be an extreme calculation because some of them may be sold sooner or later to recoup some losses. But excluding them from being counted as bad debts does raise the suspicion that regional officials were trying to cover up the true extent of the banking problems and cheat their way out of painful bank restructuring.

In particular, despite successful debt restructuring stories like Srithai Superware, Thailand has been manipulating bad debt numbers to make the headlines look good. Most of Thailand's debt is sitting in local commercial banks who have reported that their non-performing loans have dropped to 10% of their total loan assets from the near-50% levels after the 1997/1998 regional debacle. However, this figure was calculated by pushing a roughly equal amount of bad debts into the Thailand Asset Management Company and by rescheduling a similar number of loans so that they appear to be performing. If one adds these fudged dud loans, then non-performing loans hardly dropped between 2001, when the headline number was 485 billion baht, and 2002 when it was about 470 billion baht. The problem with this cheating is that the unresolved bad debt will hamper the ability of Thai firms to make fresh investments, to withstand future financial shocks, and to reposition themselves for the new paradigm.

Indeed, resolving Asia's bad loan problem will not be easy because Asian banks have rated personal relationships higher than running a market-oriented business. Further, carrying out tough reforms will undoubtedly hit bank balance sheets significantly, raising the risk of bankrupty, as banks write off the value of distressed assets. With regards to those asset management companies, they were set up as an immediate response to the 1997/1998 Asian crisis. They lack a mandate to resolve new credits that have gone bad. They also lack the ability to sell off the distressed assets, due to Asia's insufficient legal and institutional framework for bad debt sales in the secondary market. The 30% bad-debt recovery rate that McKinsey estimated earlier is probably the best rate Asia could have achieved, with future distressed assets expected to be recovered at a significantly lower rate. Further, in many cases, the underlying causes of Asia's banking problems persist. The cosy relations between Asia's bankers and borrowers continue to ensure that if borrowers run into trouble, banks will respond either by rolling over their loans or by granting concessions on interest rates.

The absence of serious corporate restructuring has also posed a big problem for banking reform due to many Asian banks' dominant exposure to the corporate sector. For example, it is true that South Korea's banking reform had a very strong start in 1999 and 2000. Non-performing loans dropped sharply as South Korean banks wrote off or sold bad debts and made large loan-loss provisions. Many banks had also redirected lending to the consumer sector, including the lucrative mortgage business, from the conglomerates. The change broadened their business scope and improved their risk profile and profit outlook.

However, these South Korean reform efforts were proven short-lived. Following the rising trend of regional non-performing loans, South Korea's bad debt surged back to 21% of total bank assets at the end of 2001. The reacceleration of bad debt accumulation reflected the deep-rooted legacy of government-directed lending in the economic bubble years of the 1980s and early 1990s. The politicised banking system has reduced banks' ability and willingness to transform themselves thoroughly. While South Korean banks have generally broadened their business scope to the consumer and mortgage segments, the bulk of their loans is still concentrated in a small group of conglomerates. Vested interests remain strong in resisting thorough cleansing of the system.

Indeed, these banking reform problems are prevalent in Asia. When it comes to the inaction of tackling bad loans, it is hard to surpass Indonesia and Thailand, whose bad debts climbed to 60% and 45% of total assets, respectively, in 2001. These economies generally have a lot of bad loans in the system because insufficient corporate restructuring has impaired companies' ability to service and repay their loans, thus keeping credit risk high in the system.

Indonesian banks were hit harder than any other Asian banks during the crisis, yet the country has been the slowest to deal with the problems. As a result, a large pile of industrial assets is still stacked up in the misnamed Indonesian Bank Restructuring Agency (IBRA). With bad debts remaining unresolved and the IBRA's inability to sell off bad bank assets, liquidity in the banking system remains constrained. It is hard for sound business to get fresh capital under these circumstances.

Further, many banks in Southeast Asia cannot rely on consumer credit, which normally has lower risk than corporate credit, to keep going. This is because personal loans and credit cards account for a very small percentage of total banking assets. For example, personal credit accounts for only 3% of total bank loans in Thailand. Mortgages, another low-risk loan asset, are also tiny in most Southeast Asian bank loan books. So, these banks would not be truly restored to health until corporate lending picks up again. But the region's broken corporate sectors will prevent this from happening in any meaningful way in the short term.

Southeast Asia also has serious problems of political interference (see next section for more) and broken court systems, which give little assurance to creditors and investors for their asset claims and ownership. These problems are supposed to be rectified as part of the structural reforms if Asian governments had really learnt from the lessons of the regional debacle. But evidence shows that they have not. A notable example was the Manulife saga in Indonesia, which, with its twists and turns of legal disputes coinciding with government-to-government intervention, must make the less-influential, normal businesses nervous. The two-month-old saga was concluded in June 2002, when the Indonesian Supreme Court overturned the bankruptcy ruling handed down earlier to the country's fourth largest life insurer – the Canadian-controlled Asuransi Jiwa Manulife Indonesia. But the damage to investor confidence in Asian reforms was done!

The company was solvent and turned in a profit of 75 billion rupiah (US$8.5 million) in 2001. But it was declared bankrupt by the Indonesian court in the midst of a lengthy dispute between Canada's Manulife Financial and its former partner at the Asuransi Jiwa Manulife joint venture. The bankruptcy action was initiated because Asuransi Jiwa Manulife did not pay a dividend in 1999. The company simply did not declare a dividend that year. The court's decision may sound ridiculous in the developed world, but obviously not paying a dividend was sufficient grounds for the Indonesian judge to rule a company bankrupt!

The Indonesian Dharmala Group originally owned Asuransi Jiwa. The saga began when Manulife entered into a joint venture with Dharmala by buying 40% of Asuransi Jiwa in a government auction of the assets of failed banks. But after the deal, a British Virgin Islands company called Roman Gold surfaced to lodge a claim based on prior ownership of the assets. When Roman Gold's claim failed, a receiver of the Dharmala Group launched an action to put Asuransi Jiwa Manulife into bankruptcy on the basis of the absence of a dividend payment. Manulife of Canada claimed that both Roman Gold and the receiver were associated with the Dharmala Group. And in the midst of the proceedings, the fireworks included a senior Asuransi Jiwa Manulife executive being mysteriously detained by police, and an individual supposedly linked to the Dharmala Group being charged with falsifying documents relating to the Roman Gold transaction. The incident was so messy that even journalists found it confusing to follow and report.

After several weeks of heated diplomatic exchanges between the Canadian and Indonesian governments, the confusing incident was settled by the Indonesian Supreme Court overturning the Asuransi Jiwa Manulife bankruptcy ruling. But the damage was done irreparably! The incident seems to prove to investors that you have to be backed by powerful forces, like a government of significant weight, to get judgements that make sense in the real world. It also highlights the inherent credibility problems of the Indonesian government in managing a economy. Consistent and reliable law enforcement and judiciary are crucial elements in building that credibility. These institutional and legal underpinnings are key to instill confidence in investors that they have inviolable property rights and creditor recourse. But the Manulife saga has exposed the dark side of Asia's piecemeal reform, as the problems in Indonesia are also reflective of similar problems in many other Southeast Asian governments.

Likewise, nobody in Thailand is sure what claims a creditor really holds until the courts are through their prolonged and confusing procedures. A series of bankruptcy reforms was beginning to take hold when the government set up its asset management company in 2001 and tried to centralise the collection of bad debts. But after embracing the idea initially, many private bankers have given up hope on chasing their claims and backed away since the reformed bankruptcy law is still inadequate for protecting creditors' rights.

Malaysia has made an effort to clean up corporate debts by pushing through some mergers, acquisitions, and consolidation deals that look quite different from the Indonesian and Thai approaches. But the government remains a key force in meddling with the business decisions. By continuing to mix business with politics, Malaysia's government will not be able to rebuild much of the long-term investor confidence that it lost during the crisis.

Following from these incidences, the question is clear: Amid all the stories of positive changes in Asia after the regional crisis, where are the fundamental reforms that are supposed to strengthen Asia's economic structure and regain investor confidence?

Structural Flaws

What all this shows is that Asia was not willing to dismantle political patronage in its economic system. As a result, crony capitalism remains a serious problem in many Asian economies.

Under the crony capitalist model, Asia governments have aggressively pursued an outward-orientation program. They either lured foreign direct investment into the export sector, as notably seen in Southeast Asia, or fostered the creation of local conglomerates, as typically seen in South Korea and to some extent Taiwan.

In Southeast Asia, political patronage in the external sector (the sector in the economy that engages in foreign trade) was the key to success in the years before the regional crisis. Since foreign multinational companies dominated the manufacturing sector that generated the bulk of export income and employment, many regional governments actually encouraged a so-called rent-seeking corporate culture based on political patronage in the local economy. The rent-seeking activities had manifested themselves in nepotism via a triangular government-bank-corporate crony complex. This triangular relationship dictated the allocation of business privileges and opportunities to favoured entrepreneurs, fostering unfair competition. Politicians and favoured enterprises appropriated and shared these economic rents, or unfair protected profits, from lucrative businesses and foreign trade. Local banks and foreign financial institutions were all part of this selfish relationship-based economic complex. They channeled large amounts of money to support this crony capitalism, fostering and sustaining production that led to excess capacity and uncompetitive businesses until the Asian crisis erupted.

The above growth dynamics was relatively simple. All that mattered was political connection. It did not require very competitive people to stay at the top. But that model is now in big trouble. Foreign funds that left in 1997/1998 will not return with force until Asia has shown renewed competitiveness. The rise of China's giant production power has complicated Asia's struggle for revival by forcing down tradable goods prices, eroding pricing power, and squeezing profit margins. Five years after the collapse of Asia's currency regimes in 1997, the region is still searching for an effective way to purge the massive unproductive investment accumulated in the pre-crisis boom. But there has not been enough will and effort to dismantle Asia's crony capitalism.

Most firms in Southeast Asia have restructured only under

duress. Businesses that have emerged solvent from the regional crisis see little reason to change their habits. Those that went bankrupt blame their governments, speculators, and the meddling of the IMF but not their crony practices. Although there are perceived efforts to shape up, Asian politics and nepotism continue to cast a shadow over business. For example, despite her seemingly radical effort to reform, Malaysia still tolerates murky business practices to protect vested interests. In 2001, the country sold a stake in the post office without any sort of public tender. Such opacity reveals the prevalence of cronyism, despite Malaysia's corporate reform efforts. Further, the government's long-standing Bumiputra Policy, which favours ethnic Malay businessmen who have connections with the government at the expense of other ethnic groups, has been a major obstacle to Malaysia's structural reforms.

In late 2002, Malaysia's Prime Minister Dr Mahathir Mohamad, due to step down in 2003, indicated that the Bumiputra Policy might no longer apply as his government strives to reform the economy. However, it is unlikely that this deep-rooted native Malay policy could be undone within a short time to make room for further economic changes. With powerful vested interests involved, tough reform initiatives are easier said than done. Look no further than Japan to see the logic of this. In April 2001, the reform-minded Junichiro Koizumi swept into office with record-high popularity as Japan's prime minister by promising drastic reforms to revive the sick economy. But after 18 months in the office with several cabinet reshuffles, Koizumi is still fighting a losing battle against the reactionary forces (see Chapter 5 for more discussion). If Koizumi, who has a much stronger reform reputation and tack record than Mahathir, cannot overcome the vested interests, it is less likely that a native Malay government would undo the Bumiputra Policy to bring about drastic economic changes in Malaysia in the short term.

In Thailand, where reform efforts are seen as the strongest among the Southeast Asian economies, the picture is mixed at best. Most listed firms now have independent directors, and a revised bankruptcy law in 2002 has helped to resolve some of the country's bad corporate debt problems. But the independent directors are frustrated with and restricted in their powers.

Personal politics still stand in the way of normal business practice. Listed companies continue to do relationship business. For example, in 2002, giant Thai construction firm BECL bought a 15% stake of Bangkok's unfinished subway from its affiliate, Charoen Karnchang. The affiliate is both an investor and a contractor in the project, underscoring the problems of cronyism and conflict of interest. Meanwhile, the new bankruptcy law remains insufficient in assuring creditors of their rights and claims by going after debtors. Many creditors have backed away from fighting for their claims shortly after the introduction of the law.

The worst abuse of cronyism can be found in Indonesia where the courts remain corrupt and unpredictable. Firms would change the dates and venues of annual meetings to awkward times and places just to frustrate those shareholders who challenge dubious and crony practices. Politics has also stymied attempts to reform big businesses. The country's IBRA has been under such pressure since its inception after the Asian crisis that it has had more than seven bosses in four years. Political connections and corruption have ensured that none of the tycoons who stole billions of dollars of banking reform funds has ever been prosecuted. The only person to have been tried in that fund cheating affair was the central bank governor; he was found guilty but nevertheless remained in his position until further notice!

Strong reluctance to change the old business model is seen even in some of the more progressive economies in Southeast Asia, like Singapore. After the regional crisis, the Singapore government has realised that it needs to change its state-directed "parental" capitalism approach after nearly four decades of micro-managing its people to create one of Asia's most disciplined and prosperous societies. Thus, in late 2001, the government formed the Economic Review Committee to remake the Lion City's economy. It also announced that it would reduce its "visible hand" in handling economic affairs by reducing the role of government-linked corporations (or GLCs). In particular, it said it would restructure its investment arm, Temasek Holdings, which controls almost every major business, including ports, banks, airlines, telecoms, property, chipmakers, media, shipping, and utilities.

In a series of policy comments between late 2001 and mid-2002, the government sent out signals that there would be significant and rapid divestment in Temasek's portfolio. In May 2002, it appointed Singapore's most powerful female leader Ho Ching as executive director of Temasek to carry out major restructuring efforts. Ho is the former head of defence contractor Singapore Technologies and daughter-in-law of Senior Minister Lee Kuan Yew; she is married to Senior Minister Lee's son, Finance Minister Lee Hsien Loong. The government might want to create the impression that the appointment was a positive move to shake up Temasek since Ho was supposed to have the necessary political clout to make changes. So Singaporeans were set up to expect big changes directed by their government.

However, the unveiling of the long-waited new charter for Temasek only went off with a whimper in July 2002. The three-page document from Temasek Holdings spelled out that little of substance would change. GLCs were sorted into two groups, those deemed strategically essential (Group A) and those which could be pushed to expand into international and regional markets (Group B). Both groups would be cultivated, not divested as many were led to believe earlier. The definition of these two groups is so broad that it only guarantees cosmetic changes. In particular, many large and non-listed GLCs fall into Group A, including media, water, power, transport, and airports. Many non-Group A category GLCs are already in Group B, and most of these GLCs have been building up their overseas businesses in recent years. This means that they would not be divested since they are deemed to possess international and regional potential under the new Temasek Charter. Existing GLCs that have not much international or regional potential will be tempted to grow a presence overseas so that they can eschew divestment also.

To a large extent, the new Temasek Charter is the "licence" for GLCs to carry out a mandated external expansion mission. Many GLC managers will thus resist divestment and favour expansion overseas as a means of keeping the status quo. In a nutshell, the government's strategy to "remake" Singapore seems to rest on using GLCs to expand overseas while clinging onto the old model that encompasses all the other industries that it deems strategic.

The mismatch between the reality of policy continuity from the Temasek, which controls 13% of the city-state's economy, and widespread expectations of a break with the past underscores the problem of reform inertia. It dissipates hopes that the appointment of high-power Ho Ching was to effect changes. Indeed, Ho's political status and connections cut both ways. She could be courageous and ready for action. Or she could keep to old way and remain inaction. The nagging problem is Singapore's fundamental impulse to control. The government regulates everything from chewing gum to requiring individuals to get permits for expressing their views at the designated Speaker's Corner.

The very dominance of the GLCs is the hallmark of the government's commanding influence in the economy. In a society where the influence of the government is so pervasive and where it is commonplace for people to look to the government for solutions to problems, the lack of political will to change is not surprising. The "parental" and controlled system only encourages conservatism and stifles an entrepreneur spirit to create a vibrant private sector. Indeed, Singapore's reform inertia is also reflective of the unwillingness of the public sector to forgo control, and hence the continuation of cronyism that is prevalent in many other Asian economies.

In a nutshell, Asia's rejuvenation depends on genuine competitiveness in the new economic paradigm. However, that requires changing people at the top of the corporate ladder. The old crowd specialises in bribing politicians. To survive in the new era, the new leadership must embrace global competition and discard cronyism. Unfortunately, the old crowd still has sufficient clout to hang onto their power. Reform suffers as a result.

Had Asia pursued tough reforms to purge its economic excess and structural woes, investment efficiency and profitability should have improved. But overall macroeconomic evidence does not exist to support the patchy anecdotal evidence of improvement in corporate profits. Indeed, overall investment efficiency remains poor in Asia. While the Asian recession in 1997/1998 did remove some economic excesses, through elimination of non-viable businesses, the region's overall investment efficiency has not risen. Figure 2.1 helps to illustrate this point clearly. It shows the marginal return on investment for Northeast and Southeast Asia. Since by definition, higher marginal return means higher income per extra unit of investment, the ratio of the change in output to the change in investment can be used as a proxy of aggregate investment efficiency. As evident from the data in Figure 2.1, there was a sharp, but only brief, jump in investment efficiency in 1998 and 1999. The rise was not sustained despite significant reduction in Asia's capital stock and investment during the regional crisis.

Another sign of the post-crisis chronic excess capacity problem comes from corporate profits squeeze. If the Asian crisis had really purged the financial and economic excesses, the sharp economic rebound and fall in interest rates that followed the crisis should generate a strong recovery in profits. But again, economy-wide macro data do not conform to anecdotal evidence of improvement. If we use the consumer price index (CPI) as an aggregate proxy for sale prices and the producer price index (PPI) as an aggregate proxy for costs, the gap between these two price indices becomes an aggregate proxy for corporate profits. This gap in Asia has been narrowing since the regional crisis, as clearly seen in the declining trend in Figure 2.2. The declining trend suggests that overall profits has not recovered, despite a

Figure 2.1   Investment Efficiency in Asia 1980–2000

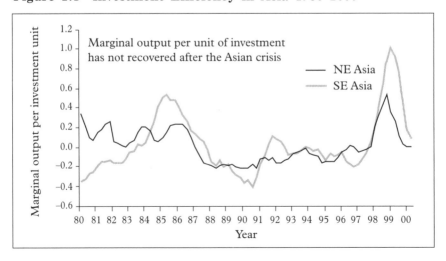

Figure 2.2 Profit Squeeze in Asia 1994–2000

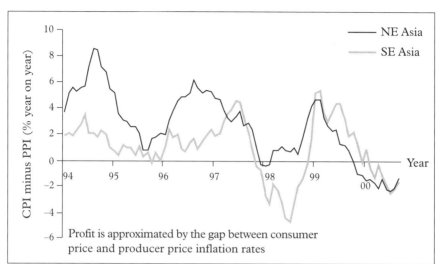

strong output rebound between 1999 and 2000. The main reason for this "profitless economic recovery" is the steady erosion of pricing power due to rising competition, especially from low-cost China, excess supply, and weak export demand.

Poor investment returns and the lack of profit growth are clear symptoms of persistent excess capacity in Asia. As for the anecdotal evidence of profit improvement in the region, it is not the result of revenue growth under a deflationary environment. Instead, it is the result of cost-cutting measures like layoffs, plant closures, and reduction in investment and other spending. But this process of boosting profits without pricing power is unsustainable because it is a process of wealth destruction – a typical symptom of a deflation environment. There is only so much a company can cut. Continued cost-cutting on the back of deflation will only darken employment and business outlook, hurt confidence and eventually private spending. Hence, an oversupply resulting from insufficient reform will continue to weigh on Asia's growth for a long time.

Further, Asia's banking systems remain malfunctioned. As discussed above, most Asian banks are still stuck with a large number of non-performing loans averaging over 20% of the size of the economy. This high bad debt ratio has continued to impair the ability of Asia's banking systems to allocate capital from savings to investment. Despite ample liquidity, the regional banks are unable and unwilling to lend due to intensifying pressure from regulators and shareholders to repair their balance sheets. In particular, banks have had to set aside more capital to provide for the high bad debt burden, thus leaving lesser funds available for lending and investment. Over-expansion during the bubble years in the 1980s and early 1990s also means that banks would have to shrink their balance sheets by reducing lending and investment to rein in excess capacity in the post-bubble years. Last but not least, the lack of improvement in credit risk due to insufficient corporate reforms acts as a major deterrent to banks' willingness to lend.

Thus, it was robust external demand, mainly from the US market and domestic public sector spending, but not credit creation, that powered Asia's post-crisis economic recovery. The depth of the region's financial woes and the resultant malfunctioned banking systems suggest that credit growth would remain subdued in Asia for many years. High debt, bad banks, and erosion of pricing power (or deflation) will remain major risks to Asia's economic growth as it moves into a new economic paradigm under the shadow of China (see next chapter).

It is likely that Asia will not be in a hurry to change its now defunct economic model. This is because the political and economic platform has allowed and encouraged the rise of crony capitalists. However, despite the detriments they pose, these crony capitalists are not masterminds of the regional economic bubble. They are mostly collaborators of past excesses. In other words, they are by-products rather than creators of Asia's political economy that allow the powerful, connected, and privileged groups to reap the lion share of wealth without bearing the corresponding burden of economic risks. They have indulged in political patronage and appropriated and shared huge economic benefits with politicians because that is the rule of the game pursued by the ruling elite. This elite group is the real mastermind of the economic excesses. As long as there are significant political vested interests in the economy, there is a lack of political will to change, and crony capitalism will continue to plague Asia.

Global Equilibrium Upset

More crucially, the trouble with Asia cheating on reforms is that an increasingly tough global environment would bode ill for Asia's structural changes to go forward. Thus, the pains from economic retrenchment would continue to haunt the region's growth in the years to come. Indeed, the sharp fall in Asia's asset prices after the bursting of the global investment bubble in mid-2001 reflects more than a cyclical correction of Asia's economic woes. It underscores the strong secular deflationary forces that are unfolding both from supply and demand.

On the supply side, China's rising production power will continue to flood the world with cheap quality products, aggravating Asia's excess capacity problem. On the demand side, the global economy is entering a prolonged period of constrained demand growth, which bodes ill for Asia's export growth. These forces will act like pliers clamping down on Asia by eroding its pricing power, profit growth, investment incentive, and employment and, hence, demand growth for many years. The phenomenon is unprecedented. It will surprise many, especially those who still indulge in the fantasy of cyclical recoveries, lifting Asian economies back to the good old days of robust growth, easy money, and fast profits.

The long global economic expansion in the 1990s has created excess demand in the developed world, notably in the US, especially during the second half of the decade. Strong productivity growth in the US and excess supply in Asia and elsewhere in the world have checked the excess demand pressure and kept inflation at bay. But this is going to change. Not that inflation will surge again, but with demand pressure falling in the medium term and no sign of excess supply receding, the global equilibrium will be upset. Deflationary forces are going to dominate.

Increasing trade and globalisation are also intensifying competitive pressure to an unprecedented extent, exerting downward pressure on global prices. The deflationary pressure is most noticeable in tradable goods prices. It is seeping into overall price levels through international trade, eroding pricing power, and squeezing corporate profits. Thus, despite the sharp and strong output rebound after the Asian financial crisis, overall profit recovery in Asia has remained subdued. Excess capacity and intense competition have forced manufacturers to cut prices in the face of constrained demand. This phenomenon is going to last for a much longer period than many people would expect, as the deflationary forces that Asia, and the global economy, is facing are unprecedented.

Skeptics would argue that aggressive interest rate cuts by national central banks could help restore the global balance by boosting demand so that Asia's growth would also benefit. This may not necessarily be the case anymore. The effectiveness of global monetary policy has been, and will continue to be, blunted by the lack of inflation and impaired balance sheets of banks, corporates, and consumers. The textbook logic of lower interest rates boosting private sector demand may not come through in reality when the monetary transmission is broken, as is the case in Asia. When consumers and companies are heavily indebted, they are unable to finance any further spending via borrowing. Poor consumer and corporate balance sheets also mean high credit risk, which in turn deters banks to lend. Large bad debts also weigh on the lending ability of banks. Lastly, the combination of debt and deflation erodes economic confidence and drags on private spending and demand for credit. In all these cases, interest rates become an irrelevant variable in affecting spending.

In the US, the largest export market for Asia, the Federal Reserve's aggressive monetary easing in 2001 and 2002 pushed interest rates to historic lows. This allowed US businesses to recover from the profit recession and helped prevent a devastating financial accident in the US banking system. On a positive note, the Federal Reserve's aggressive policy move thus helped minimise the negative impact of the US systemic risk on the global economy at a time when different economic zones entered a synchronised slowdown. However, this does not mean that US investments would surge anytime soon because profits would remain under secular stress (see the next chapter), dampening investment incentive. From a structural-adjustment point of view, the shallow US economic recession in 2001 might not be good news as the rapid policy stimulation by the US authorities has halted the economic cleansing process. In other words, the economic and financial excesses of the 1990s were being masked but not eliminated. The prevalence of excesses will drag economic growth in the coming years.

Excessive greed and hype about future business outlook had generated supply gluts, excessive borrowing, and over-investment, causing the profit collapse in the late 1990s and early 2000s. All these were economic woes grown from within the global economic system. Thus, to restore profitability, these excesses must be eliminated by bringing income and profit expectations back down to reality. In other words, the global system will have to go through a process of balance sheet retrenchment, with banks cutting bad debts and reducing lending, and corporates and consumers repaying their debts and cutting spending. This will inevitably result in a prolonged period of slow growth. Economic stimulants, such as expansionary fiscal and monetary policies or lower oil prices, will help restore corporate profitability, but only temporarily. Until the structural excesses of oversupply and excessive debt are resolved, they will not be decisive factors for sustaining profits growth in the long term.

All this means that the global system would be stuck with constrained economic growth, stubborn oversupply pressure and intensifying competition for many years. These factors will unleash strong deflationary forces, creating waves of liquidation pressure on suppliers. Such a global backdrop will only aggravate Asia's structural pains, dragging on its domestic demand and forcing it to rely on exports for growth. But export-led growth will not be an optimal model for Asia anymore (see Chapter 8). New business models and pricing strategies will have to be designed in order to succeed under an increasing hostile economic environment driven by China's rising economic might. Meanwhile, Asian exporters will be hard pressed to slash prices to compete for stagnant, or even shrinking, export demand. Thus, before the Asian economic transformation is completed, many Asian exchange rates will come under long-term downward pressure, as the region seeks an escape route to growth via currency depreciation during the onset of the new economic paradigm.

Chapter 3

China Shapes the New Economic Paradigm

Long gone are the good old days of fast economic growth and easy money made from surging asset prices in the regional markets. What follows in the coming years in Asia will likely be a new economic era with subdued profits, constrained demand growth, weak pricing power, and secular weakness for some Asian asset prices and currencies. The persistence of these macroeconomic trends will surprise many because the breadth and depth of these forces have not been seen before. Asia is moving into a new economic paradigm of rising competition, disinflation and restricted economic growth. The changes are partly a result of Asia's inevitable economic adjustment to an integrated world economy after the bursting of its economic bubble. They are also partly a result of the rising economic might of China. In essence, Asia's post-bubble transformation reflects the much needed structural adjustment to reduce excess capacity. Meanwhile, the rise of China as a giant production force highlights the source of deflationary pressures amid this adjustment process.

The legacy of excessive investment of the 1990s will linger for many years. Capital investment growth in the US, for example, outpaced gross domestic product (GDP) growth by an average of 65% in the 1990s. This caused a surge in the US investment-to-GDP ratio similar to Asia's over-investment build-up in the run up to the 1997/1998 regional crisis. Meanwhile, Asia's excess capacity has not been eliminated (see Chapter 2).

Prolonged global competition and a sharp rise in trade penetration by developing countries, notably China, in the world export market are exerting long-term downward pressures on prices, nominal growth, and corporate earnings. China's rising production power will intensify these inherent deflationary forces in the new economic paradigm.

Debt Deflation: Troubles Ahead

All this excess capacity will remain a dominant force for curbing inflation for a long time. While inflation is normally seen as an evil because it erodes living standards by eroding real purchasing power, the lack of inflation will be equally bad, at least at the onset of the new paradigm. This is because the lack of global inflation will become a drag on the heavily indebted consumer and corporate sectors, whose debt burden will not be eroded by inflation. Thus, due to the poor shape of private sector balance sheets in the major economies, excess demand pressure that existed in the 1990s is unlikely to emerge anytime soon (see Chapter 8). This removes major support for global pricing power and constitutes a significant secular dragging force on corporate profits. Oversupply and feeble demand raise the risk of a vicious debt-deflation cycle. In such a situation, falling prices raise the debt burden and hurt spending power. Weak demand in turn weakens prices and raises the debt burden further, thus creating a vicious cycle. No economy can sustain a robust recovery under the deadly combination of debt and deflation!

United States consumers, who are the largest customer base for Asian exports, were the buyers of last resort for Asian products in the 1990s. Their robust demand helped sustain Asia's economic growth, especially after the Asian crisis. But any hope of the American consumer returning to their buying binge in the coming years will be unrealistic due to their heavy debt burden that will drag down their spending power for years. Behind America's surging stock market and economic bubble in the 1990s was a private sector borrowing binge. This debt craze was based on the overly optimistic expectations that rapid growth in profits, share prices, and wages would go on forever. The huge build-up of private sector debt financed the boom in investment and consumer spending. The stock market bubble has popped since 2001 and the information technology investment boom has turned to bust. But the American credit bubble remains inflated. Only when it deflates will the dampening impact on spending be felt completely not only in the US, but also across Asia as US import demand dries up.

The US consumer balance sheets are overstretched, and thus their spending habit of mortgaging future income to finance current consumption is unsustainable. Eventually, creditors and debtors will wake up to the reality that their expectations of future income and profit growth were too rosy. Consumers will have to cut back on spending to bring their debt load back to sustainable levels. However, unwinding America's heavy debt burden, which amounted to US$32 trillion in combined public and private debt in 2001, could take longer this time than before. This is because in previous excessive borrowing, inflation had quickly eroded the real debt burden, allowing big spenders off the hook. But this time, the US economy is facing prolonged global deflationary pressures so that the real debt burden will remain heavy. Hence, the drag on demand growth will remain large for years.

This means that global nominal GDP growth would be weak and there would not be any significant inflationary threat for a long time. It also means that pricing power would be capped. Since profit growth correlates closely with nominal GDP growth, global corporate profits would come under stress when there is no pricing power. This will, in turn, erode investment incentive. While profits will still recover as the global economic cycle revives, the recovery pace will be much more subdued than many investors would expect. The lack of pricing power also means that any profit growth would have to come from cost-cutting. But this way of boosting business margins is deflationary, with an undesirable effect of wealth destruction – shrinking business, falling asset prices, and rising unemployment. This process could trap the global economy below potential growth for a long time, like in Japan where GDP growth has averaged about 1% since her asset bubble burst in the early 1990s.

Productivity growth usually rises sharply at the onset of an economic recovery, as firms are slow to hire new workers. This helps lower unit labour cost while sales volume grows, hence boosting corporate margins. However, faster productivity growth does not necessarily translate into fatter profits now because firms' bottom lines also depend on the pricing environment. Technological advancement, especially Information Technology (IT) development, allows companies to cut costs. But it also lowers industry entry barriers and information cost. This makes markets more transparent, and thus increasing competition and eroding pricing power. Companies will end up being forced to pass those cost savings onto consumers instead of reaping them in increased profits. This, along with global excess capacity, will squeeze profit margins even if output growth rebounds robustly.

For the first time since the 1930s, the world is facing the problem of too little inflation but not rampant price increases. Indeed, given the structural problems of high debt and oversupply, it is very likely that the global economy will be plagued by periods of deflation amid a prolonged period of disinflation. But global authorities have yet to fully understand the deflation syndrome and hence have not been able to prescribe any effective policies to control it. Excess capacity, the absence of pricing power, and persistent unemployment will be the hallmarks of the new economic paradigm in the global system. The corporate reengineering philosophy of debt-financing business expansion of the 1980s and 1990s will be replaced by the new reengineering measures of debt reduction and business cutbacks in the years to come.

Formidable China

Aggravating these deflationary forces is the rise of China's economic might, notably through her production of cheap quality products that are sweeping through the global market. Entry to the World Trade Organisation (WTO) will help consolidate China's competitive power, which will in turn impart more deflationary forces across Asia, albeit to differing degrees. China's competitive power can be readily seen in the fact that despite being outside the WTO and withstanding the pressure of currency devaluation during the 1997/1998 Asian crisis, Chinese exports recovered sharply after it. Using statistics from the CEIC data bank, evidence shows that China's export market share in the US has risen to 24% of US imports from the Pacific Rim from less than 20% in 1997. But the aggregate export market share of the Association of Southeast Asian Nations (ASEAN) has shrunk to less than 20% from 23% despite rounds of currency devaluation.

The Middle Kingdom is learning to make the same products as the "tiger" economies (South Korea, Hong Kong, Taiwan, and Singapore) did in the 1980s, but at a much faster pace. Chinese labour cost, on the other hand, is merely a fraction of the "tigers'" then. Further, China's labour force is seven times as large as that of Japan and the "tiger" economies combined. However, China's labour cost, which is still the lowest in Asia except Indonesia, is only one factor that makes her competitive. The Mainland is suffering from excess capacity, which remains stubbornly large despite steady inventory reduction since the Asian crisis. But this structural weakness has ironically turned out to be another force helping China's external competitiveness. This is because the combination of oversupply pressure from inventory liquidation and low labour cost has prompted the Chinese manufacturers to slash export prices. This has in turn exerted strong competitive pressures on neighbouring economies. China's supply pressure and labour cost advantages are likely to remain intact in the coming years, threatening Asia with more competitive stress.

Efficiency, the essence of competitiveness, is achieved through competition. Many are surprised to hear that improving efficiency also applies to China. Looking deeper, it is evident that competition is happening in China, despite the bureaucracy and the nuisance of the state sector. China's competition arises from a unique combination of excess capacity and profit incentive. There are just too many people looking for work, keeping wages down. There are also too many suppliers looking for buyers, keeping prices down. While this is part of China's excess capacity symptom, it underlines keen competition on the back of a drive to search for profits in the domestic economy. Thus, whenever a market becomes profitable, thousands of firms flock into this market in a short time, eroding away any excess profits. This is why profitability in China has remained generally low, but companies are becoming more efficient than ever before through competition. Because of these forces, China is emerging as the centre where global prices are determined.

Even developed economies are feeling China's heat. For example, China is already challenging Japanese exports. The Chinese export structure has shifted steadily towards higher value-added goods, such as electronics and machinery, and away from low value-added primary goods. Statistics from the CEIC data bank provide strong evidence for this structural shift in China's exports. In 1994, low-value manufacturing goods accounted for about 20% of China's total exports, while electronics and machinery accounted for about 17% of the total. In less than ten years, this export mix has changed dramatically. By 2001, the share of low value-added products had dropped to 10% of China's total exports, while the share of high value-added products had risen to 35%. This structural shift is also an evidence of China's engagement in structural reforms by switching production expenditure to high value-added exports from sunset industries.

Reflecting China's challenge to Japan is her trade surplus with the US, which has surpassed Japan's since 2000. The rise in Japanese protectionism in recent years against many Chinese imports, ranging from manufactured goods and textile to primary products such as vegetables, in turn reflects Japan's deep concern about China's competitive threat. There is an irony about the Japanese protectionist measures. After the initial wave of expansion into China for her vast domestic market in the late 1980s, Japanese firms are rediscovering China as a cheap production base for exports back to Japan. Thus, many of the products on Japan's protection list are actually made by Japanese subsidiaries in China. While this phenomenon makes the game of international trade more confusing, it underscores China's rising economic clout in the global production stage.

With her push into higher value-added output, China even sets her sights on the high-tech sector. She has become the newest player in IT outsourcing. Expectations are high for China to challenge India's dominant position in IT outsourcing and become an export powerhouse for software and IT services in the next few years. When a company thinks about outsourcing its

IT needs, it naturally thinks of India first due to her cheap and quality services backed by a large pool of software engineers. The country has thus built a thriving software industry based on demand from overseas buyers for programming that is cheaper than what they can get at home. But as rising demand pushes against capacity constraint, diminishing returns set in and push up Indian prices. Thus, opportunities are opening for the entry of newer, lower-cost competitors.

China is ready to take a shot, with 300,000 software professionals and 30,000 new graduates every year. Wages are 15%–20% below Indian levels and a mere 17% of US rates. These comparative advantages could make China the next frontier for the offshore IT market. Indeed, the industry is expecting China to become one of the world's top offshore outsourcing hot spots between 2007 and 2010. The advent of China as a major player will intensify the competitive pressure in the already transparent and highly competitive IT industry. Since the IT development is a major cause for deflationary pressure, the China factor will further curb Asia's pricing power and squeeze corporate profits in the new economic paradigm.

But this does not mean that achieving China's ambition would be smooth-sailing. Only about 10% of her IT workers have experience in complex programming tasks. Insufficient English skills also hinder communication with clients, who come mainly from North America and Europe. Organisational ability for large and complicated jobs is another handicap facing the Chinese. Then there is the thorny issue of intellectual property rights, the essence of the software business. Piracy is rampant in China, and some companies are concerned about Chinese contractors abusing confidential or proprietary data. Further, China's software export is still in its infancy, with annual exports amounting to around US$600,000, compared to India's US$6.2 billion.

The task to overcome these problems may be daunting, but they are unlikely to hold back the Middle Kingdom. Workers' experience can be accumulated, just like their English skills can be learnt. And the Chinese attitude to thrive is admirable. Learning English has become a national awareness, especially after their WTO entry, and the Chinese are trying hard with a strong resolve to succeed. Their drive contrasts sharply with the complacency and lack of vision of Hong Kong. For example, soon after the reversion of Hong Kong to China in July 1997, the Hong Kong government, in a bid to show its patriotism, decided to use "mother-tongue" as the medium of teaching. But the definition of "mother-tongue" is never clear, as it could mean using Cantonese (which is Hong Kong's local dialect) or Mandarin (China's national language). Many Mainland Chinese are surprised by Hong Kong's decision. They wonder why Hong Kong, being an international city, is going backward by de-emphasising the use of English while the Mainland is pursuing a national push to use English?

Progress in other areas could come quickly. Now that China is a WTO member, rules and regulations are being improved and/or designed to protect intellectual property rights. Crucially, rising income and the change in the Chinese mindset to embrace the world are acting to improve their attitude towards property rights. Indeed, some foreign companies are already reporting positive experiences. For example, Dotster, a US-based internet domain name registrar, used Chinese programmers to create a multilingual interface for its website. It was quite happy with the trusting experience it had with the Chinese partners and wanted to work with them again.

Other companies are using Chinese software engineers to do some of the high-end work for which India is known. For example, Objectiva, a US outsourcing company with operations in Beijing, is employing Chinese engineers to develop sophisticated business applications using Sun Microsystem's advanced business software platform, the J2EE. Meanwhile, Chinese engineers at IT United, an IT services company with operations in North America and China, have created a diverse range of applications, including a system for evaluating employee performance. These foreign companies have generally reported pleasant business and working relationships in China, evidence that counters the suspicion by some other foreign companies about China's ability to perform high value-added work. In a nutshell, it is too simple to generalise what is happening in China with anecdotes.

China is serious about catching up with, and eventually challenging, India. She has launched a series of initiatives to bolster the country's software industry. They include sending fact-finding and research delegations to India's high-tech hub, Bangalore, setting up an IT Industry Promotion Centre, and developing training programmes for corporate personnel. Before China can go on her own, she may flex her competitive muscles by teaming up with Asian partners. Hong Kong, with its better technical skills (at least in the short term) and educated young labour force, has a golden opportunity to leverage on the China IT initiatives (see Chapter 6) to reengineer its economy in the new paradigm. Meanwhile, India is taking China's ambition seriously. Some Indian companies are teaming up with Chinese firms to combine local cost savings with India's project management and superior programming skills. For example, InfoSys Technologies, India's largest IT outsourcing firm, has set up a software development centre in Shanghai to serve as a hedge against the potential downturn in India's outsourcing trade.

Pressuring Asia

China's export-push policy since the mid-1990s has already created a large downward pressure on Asia's export prices. While the Asian financial crisis in 1997 and 1998 distorted the trade and price data, the Chinese deflationary impact on the regional export pricing environment has become clear since 1999. According to national statistics provided by the CEIC data bank, Chinese export volume has been rising at an average rate of 10% a year since 1999, but Asia's export prices have been falling by an average of 4.2% a year since then. And there are no signs that this widening gap between rising Chinese export volume and falling Asian export prices would close anytime soon. This is because both the mounting competitive stress and the inherent excess capacity problem from the Mainland will act to keep tradable goods supply ample and export prices low.

WTO-induced reforms and rising competition are going to strengthen China's competitive power and curb Asia's pricing power further. This competitive stress on the regional exporters will manifest itself in downward pressure on many Asian exchange rates. Due to the economic and structural rigidities in Asia, it would be impossible for the regional economies to cut domestic cost quick enough to match the Chinese competition in a short time. Currency depreciation has thus become the fastest way for Asia to raise competitiveness by cutting export prices in one stroke across the board.

These price and currency depreciation pressures from China in fact argue against the conventional wisdom that falling Asian currencies would undermine the Chinese renminbi's (RMB) fundamentals and prompt an eventual RMB devaluation. It should be the other way round, with Chinese competition pushing down Asian currencies in an increasingly competitive environment. The evidence is clear, as shown in Figure 3.1. China started pursuing an export-push policy in the early 1990s and has successfully created a critical mass in the export industries by the mid-1990s. As a result, Chinese export volume has been rising and export prices have been falling since then. But the steady fall in China's export prices has also put downward pressure on Asian currencies. Given the persistence of China's competitive pressure, her impact on regional currencies will remain a dominant force in Asia's foreign trade environment in the new economic paradigm.

China's entry to the WTO has indeed raised concerns in Asia about a "giant sucking sound" – the term coined in 1992 by the then US Presidential candidate Ross Perot to demonise the

Figure 3.1   China's Pressure on Asian Currencies

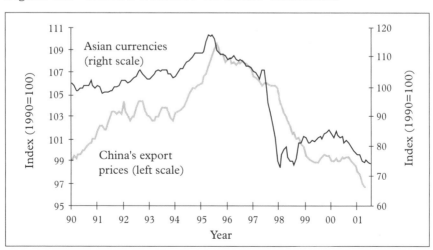

North American Free Trade Agreement (NAFTA). The alarmist Perot feared that Mexico, with her cheap cost of production, would suck away all the manufacturing jobs from the US, breaking the rice bowl of American workers. Nevertheless, it was fortunate that Perot's effort to block the NAFTA, and his bid to the US Presidency, failed because as it turned out, Mexico and the US economies were complementary in the production chain, and NAFTA benefited both.

Nevertheless, free trade does not guarantee a win-win situation for every player every time a new market is opened. Just like tax cuts in a national economy, the long-term overall impact will be positive, but the adjustment process may leave some individuals worse off in the short term. The advent of China as a global trade player is having a similar effect on a global scale. Basically, economies with an export structure similar to China's will feel most of the competitive stress. In this aspect, Thailand, the Philippines, and even (surprisingly) Taiwan will face enormous competition from China. It is obvious that Thailand and the Philippines are producing mostly low value-added exports that compete with China directly. But Taiwan's competitive stress comes mainly from the acceleration of the migration of Taiwanese manufacturing business and investment to China, a process called "hollowing out". Such acceleration is an inevitable result of the removal of the restrictions by the Taiwanese government on the island's trade with and investment in the Mainland.

Hong Kong is a prime example of potential Chinese pressure on Taiwan's future economic development. Hong Kong's manufacturers moved their production to Southern China in the early 1980s to escape high local production costs. Its whole manufacturing base was relocated to the Mainland within 15 years, leaving only the high value-added segments, such as logistics, design, and marketing, in the territory. Hong Kong has succeeded in rejuvenating itself into a financial and services centre, thanks to its strong entrepreneurial spirit and unique geographical and political positions.

Taiwanese manufacturers are going through the same pressure due to the erosion of export pricing power and rising competition. With high domestic production costs, Taiwanese manufacturers have to find a cheap production base to survive the competition. China is a natural choice due to her cultural and language similarities with Taiwan and geographical proximity. Even Taiwan's strong electronics industry is accelerating its relocation of manufacturing facilities to China. But the transformation process is not as certain for Taiwan as it was for Hong Kong in the 1980s. This is because Taiwan has to reinvent herself under the shadow of local structural problems and political complications, both internally and with the Mainland, in a new paradigm where economic hostility prevails.

Overall, Southeast Asia may bear the brunt of the adjustment process, due to the similarity between China's export structure and theirs. China's elevation up the value-added ladder could marginalise even the lowest cost producers, such as Indonesia. In the mid-1980s, Chinese and Indonesian textile industries were roughly equivalent in terms of the value-added of their products. China has since gone on to produce up-market sports and winter clothing. But Indonesian makers have not upgraded to keep pace. They have continued to produce cheap cotton garments. Keen competition from China, the lack of economies of scale and little value-added have eroded their profit margins despite cheap labour.

Indonesia's problems also highlight the risk of an economic downward spiral when Chinese competition aggravates bad domestic policies. Indeed, this risk also applies to all of Asia. Indonesia's dire manufacturing environment is notable in the shoe-making industry. According to the Indonesian Footwear Association, or Aprisindo, one-third of the country's 300 shoe manufacturers had gone under between 1999 and 2001. The whole footwear industry could be shut down by 2007 according to Aprisindo's forecast. But this prediction is probably too optimistic. A combination of disastrous government policy coming on top of rising Chinese competition would probably wipe out the industry before that.

In particular, the labour law implemented in 2002 that shortened working hours, raised employment costs, together with a steep rise in regional taxes and a 39% hike in minimum wages will lead to a steady exodus of labour intensive industries, like shoe-making, out of Indonesia. Textiles and garments will follow, quite likely moving to China, when the developed markets eliminate their textile import quotas in 2005. According to the World Bank, Chinese apparel output is expected to quadruple within ten years, flooding the global market with cheap high quality clothing and crashing low value-added producers. Meanwhile, Indonesia's toy industry has already moved to China and the furniture industry is following suit.

In other words, Indonesia has priced herself out of the market just at a time when competition from China is mounting. The Middle Kingdom's competitive edge has not come by luck. Beijing has worked hard to gain it by investing billions of dollars in improving infrastructure and pursued a balanced macroeconomic and structural reform policy mix, while Jakarta has sat on its hands. The vote of investor confidence in China is clear, with foreign direct investment inflow growing by 20% a year since the late 1990s. This contrasts sharply with the lack of confidence in Indonesia's business environment and government credibility, which has cost the country dearly. From an inflow of US$11.5 billion in 1996, foreign capital has been flowing out of Indonesia at a rate of US$10 billion a year since 1998, mostly on the concern of the country's corrupt legal system.

In general, Asia's emerging economies are particularly vulnerable to Chinese competition because they have deliberately pursued export-led growth policies at the expense of domestic consumption. To varying degrees, they have tried to follow Japan's mercantiles system, promoting high savings and directing them to conglomerates picked by governments to be national winners in the global market. This growth strategy worked well for Asia in the early stages of development. This was because the regional economies were kept more open than other countries that embraced a closed-door policy so that their industries were disciplined by global competition. But as the 1997/1998 Asian crisis and Japan's prolonged economic slump have shown, this growth model creates an emphasis on output expansion at the expense of profitability. This output-profit trade off has coupled with crony capitalism to ultimately create the economic disaster in 1997/1998. The arrival of China on the scene will drive the nails into the coffin of Asia's low-efficiency, manufacturing-based, export-led economic model in the new economic era.

Engine for Growth and Investment

While the emergence of China's economic clout will inflict competitive pains in Asia, it will also be positive for Asia's growth by being a source of demand, both directly and indirectly. The direct impact is clear. As a percentage of GDP, China already imports more than Japan, notably from Asia, though China's economy is only a quarter of the size of Japan. Indeed, China has been running a trade deficit with Asia since 2000. In 2001, China's trade deficit with Asia amounted to a monthly average of US$10 billion, a dramatic reversal from the huge monthly average surplus of US$21 billion in 1998. This deficit trend is likely to continue, as WTO opens more doors for Asian exports to China, whose import appetite will also grow under rising income growth and demand for industrial upgrading.

Indeed, China's increasingly affluent urban population is becoming the fastest-growing market for many entertainment and consumer product manufacturers in South Korea, Taiwan, and Japan. Chinese factories are also buying an increasing amount of raw materials and components from around Asia. Those factories, in turn, are pumping out products that are often reexported to Europe and the US. In other words, booming Chinese exports to developed markets also indirectly benefit other Asian suppliers who sell to China. Further, foreign-invested companies produce as much as half of China's exports. While some of these foreign investors are just Chinese businesses concealed as Hong Kong-based entities, many more are from Taiwan, South Korea, Singapore, and elsewhere in Asia. Therefore, a rise in China's exports should raise income for Asian manufacturers, thus imparting a beneficial effect across the region.

For example in Singapore, while a fast-growing China may be taking away lower-skilled jobs at a rapid rate and is dominating foreign direct investment flows, the Mainland also offers the city-state an increasingly important market. Singapore's unions estimated that more than 42,000 jobs were lost, mostly to China, between 1997 and 2001. But there are also tremendous trade benefits, which can be seen in the dramatic change in the Singapore-China trade pattern over the past decade. Bilateral trade grew at a robust rate of 15% a year between 1990 and 2000, with exports to China rising by 20% per annum and imports from China growing by 13%. More recently, total bilateral trade surged by 57% between 1997 and 2001. The steady improvement has continued every year, despite the regional crisis of 1997/1998 when two-way trade slowed to a growth rate of 3%.

At the start of the 1990s, Singapore–China trade was mostly concentrated in commodities and primary goods. Heading to China from the Lion City were mainly mineral fuels, petroleum products, chemicals, and machinery and equipment. Between them, these four product lines accounted for 92% of total trade then. Coming from China were much the same items – mineral fuels, petroleum products, chemicals, machinery equipment, and manufactured goods. But as total trade volume surges in recent years, the composition has shifted in favour of higher value-added goods. Singapore is selling to China more electronic valves, office and data machines, and sophisticated machinery and equipment.

The Singapore–China trade example highlights the importance of China both as a market for Asian exporters and as a force to effect structural changes for other economies to evolve. As China develops, trade in electronics and machinery and equipment has risen sharply throughout the 1990s, and has overtaken trade in commodities. China's abundant resources, which makes her an attractive location for labour intensive electronics manufacturing, have resulted in bigger linkages between Chinese and Singaporean electronics firms. This is part of Asia's regional division of labour in the electronics industry, with economies at different segments of the value-added chain complementing each other. Indeed, notwithstanding China's overall competitive pressure, complementarity will become a hallmark of Asia's new economic model rather than China driving out her competitors.

Economic complementarity is not limited to foreign trade; it also applies to investment flows. Contrary to common perceptions, China has not gained foreign direct investment (FDI) at the expense of the rest of Asia (see Chapter 4 for a detailed discussion). In fact, FDI inflows to Asia have risen along with inflows to China. One reason for this investment complementarity is that Asian economies are at different development stages. Thus, FDI may be drawn to different comparative advantages within the region – some to abundant labour, like China, and some to technological know-how, like South Korea, Taiwan, and Singapore. Another reason is that multinational companies often want to be closer to their customers and production partners. Hence, they have a strategic preference to place investment along the global marketing and production chain. Since Asia is a region with a dispersed marketplace and production base, FDI placement has also been diversified throughout the region.

Rising foreign investment into China is not a zero sum game. Economic ties between China and Asia are buoying intra-regional trade and investment flows. It is impossible for China to have comparative advantage in all manufacturing sectors. There is room for China and the rest of Asia to develop side by side, for instance by trading semi-finished goods to take advantage of the efficiency gains from greater division of labour between different economies. This intra-regional trade will provide a cushion for Asian exports when demand slows in other major markets, such as the US and Japan. If and when China begins to act as a continent-sized engine for Asia's growth, she will likely replace the US as the major market for Asian exports, and will eventually become a significant investor in the region. There is evidence that some Chinese firms are already investing overseas aggressively.

Haier Group, China's largest appliance company based in Qingdao, boasts manufacturing facilities in Indonesia, the Philippines, and Malaysia (as well as in Iran and the US). Other Chinese manufacturers that have gone abroad include the New Hope Group, which has invested significantly in animal feed plants in Vietnam and the Philippines, and the Holley Group (based in Hangzhou), which has invested millions of dollars in Thailand and India making electricity meters. In a landmark deal in early 2002, China's state-owned offshore oil company CNOOC bought from Spanish oil company Repsol-YPF its oil and gas assets in Indonesia for US$585 million. The deal was the biggest foreign acquisition of upstream Indonesian oil and gas assets in over ten years. Some Chinese firms are buying Indonesian timber, pulp and paper, and coal mines. Others are involved in infrastructure projects, like building roads, bridges, and railway lines in Indonesia. Even in finance, Chinese banks are setting their eyes overseas, with notably the state-owned Bank of China boasting operations in North America and Europe. It is also expanding into Jakarta after a break of over 35 years.

Chinese investment in Southeast Asia remains modest in absolute terms for now. But the potential for expansion is big, as China grows stronger economically in the coming years. The WTO is changing the Chinese mindset by prompting Chinese businesses to realise that they would have to expand beyond the Middle Kingdom and take a proactive strategy to cope with the WTO challenges. All this refutes the view that China's low cost environment would just attract investment inflow but deter local investment going abroad. Accelerating foreign investment by Chinese corporates in Asia illustrates the awakening of Chinese entrepreneurs to the global competitive challenge, and the growing self-confidence of Chinese companies in business expansion. These trends, in turn, signify increasing Chinese economic and political clout in Asia and the fading of an era when Japan and the US were the major engines for Asia's economic growth.

Push for Reform and Cooperation

More subtly, China could become a force pushing reforms in Asia. As Asian economies rebounded from the 1997/1998 regional crisis faster than expected, governments slipped on reforms. Robust economic growth eroded the will to reform and bred complacency. Firms were reluctant to sell off assets and reduce debts. Banks were slow in writing off bad loans. This failure of many regional governments to implement reforms after the Asian crisis has worsened Asia's economic drag, as weak banks and inadequate corporate restructuring have eroded the underlying power of domestic demand growth. This failure has also rendered government economic stabilisation policies ineffective. Interest rate cuts have become powerless in boosting demand, as banks saddled with bad loans are reluctant to lend more and debt-ridden corporates cannot borrow more.

Fiscal policy has not worked properly either. Japan is a prime example showing that fiscal expansion without structural reforms does not produce sustainable economic growth. Tokyo has spent over US$1 trillion since 1993 on stimulus packages, but the economy has only crawled at an annual average growth of 1.6%. This means that there had never been sufficient domestic demand to propel growth. From a reform perspective, this is also a Pan-Asia problem. It can be argued that Japan and Asia's large trade surpluses were not a sign of economic vigour. This is because they partly reflect that insufficient reforms had failed to generate strong domestic demand such that they had to rely on export demand for growth.

Notwithstanding the investment complementarity that China brings to Asia, Southeast Asia (except Singapore) runs the risk of being marginalised as a site for foreign investment. This is because the region lacks aggressive reform to regain foreign investor confidence. It also lacks the economic size and market potential of China to attract foreign investment. Beijing has pushed ahead with structural reforms, albeit at a slow pace, since the Asian crisis. But many Asian governments have failed to sustain their reform efforts. As Beijing continues to liberalise its economy, other countries will be pressed to tackle the Chinese challenge if they do not want to be left out by global investors.

Acutely aware of Asia's concerns about her economic ascent, China has attempted to assure her benefits for the region. Her most notable move to initiate economic cooperation is a raft of free trade arrangements with ASEAN, the most high profiled being the proposed China–ASEAN Free Trade Area (CSFTA), endorsed by both sides in November 2001. The free trade area is set to take shape within a decade. China's idea is to give the Southeast Asian neighbours a boost in their exports to the Chinese market. The CSFTA will offer even greater trade liberalisation than what China agreed to as part of her WTO accession agreement. For example, tariff rates within the CSFTA will be much lower, and reduced much faster, than the general commitment to the WTO.

Among those set to benefit the most will be the least-developed members of ASEAN, such as Cambodia, Myanmar,

Laos, and Vietnam, with China agreeing to extend to them the same most-favoured-nation trading status that she grants to WTO members. For Southeast Asia as a whole, Japan as an export market still dwarfs China, but only marginally. The importance of the Japanese market probably will not last for too long. National trade data provided by the CEIC data bank shows that exports from the four largest Southeast Asian economies to Japan have been declining steadily to around 15% from over 31% in 1985. This trend suggests that there would be indeed a strong need for Southeast Asia to increase their exports elsewhere. The growth of the Chinese market and the eventual advent of the CSFTA will just come in handy.

The direct benefit of the CSFTA will be increased market scope, as member economies will be free to engage in cross-border trade within the Area. But there is a subtler indirect benefit – the CSFTA will push the different regional economies to specialise in products that they have the best comparative advantage in making. During the boom years before the Asian crisis, when rising prices underpinned both the goods and asset markets, Asia pursued some sort of commune development. Infrastructure provision was limited to areas chosen by the powers and the politically connected. And these privileged areas engaged in all kinds of production and exports that the bosses decided, disregarding the strengths and weaknesses of their endowments and abilities.

This was possible when inflation made pricing power strong and profits easy without the need for manufacturers to focus on the best they could do. In other words, they did not have to be very competitive to survive. They could even thrive because the inflation tide raised all ships. However, as Asia moves into the new paradigm where deflationary forces persist, the situation will be totally different. Generalisation, like those commune development areas that do many things, will not work. Manufacturers must exploit their strongest comparative advantage and specialise to survive. The CSFTA will provide the backdrop for regional division of labour by reducing trade barriers within the Area.

China's pitch to ASEAN, in particular, has a political element as well. Given their history of territorial disputes, moves towards a free trade area are a form of political confidence booster for both China and ASEAN. It can be seen as a way for China to respond to the US "Asia policy" and find her own area for counterbalance. More subtly, the CSFTA offers a way for China to begin to challenge Japan's role as the dominant economic powerhouse in Asia. On the other hand, Japan and the US are also seeking pacts with countries in the region to counter China's overtures towards Southeast Asia. Even New Delhi is also taking steps to answer Beijing's growing influence in Southeast Asia by calling an annual India–ASEAN summit.

All these cooperation and ally-building exercises only underscore China's impact on pulling together various countries to form interest groups to survive the new paradigm. China's emergence is an undeniable fact. If Asia cannot reject it, the region will have to figure out how to face the challenges and, hopefully, turn them into opportunities. While the ultimate impact of China on Asia's economic development remains to be seen, one certainty is that Asian and global manufacturers will continue to face significant supply pressure from China. As a result, pricing power will be capped and profit growth constrained. New business models, especially for Asian corporates, and pricing strategies will have to be designed in order to succeed under the shadow of China's economic might. Meanwhile, before the Asian economic transformation is complete, many Asian exchange rates will come under downward pressure, as the regional economies seek an escape route via currency depreciation to boost exports to counter the rising Chinese competitive pressure.

On a positive note, in the new economic paradigm, China's success will spur Asia's reform efforts. Other economies lagging in reform may feel insecure or threatened, but they will also realise that they have to catch up to survive. There may be an uneven development in Asia on its road to efficiency, with specific spots of strong performance coexisting uneasily with areas of weakness. But China could well be a catalyst for improving the general level of welfare across Asia. To ensure this, countries would need to come to terms with the threats and opportunities emanating from a more internationally accessible Chinese economy.

Chapter 4

Foreign Trade and Investment — The Chinese Magnet

Some observers see the rise in China's economic power as a political and economic threat. It also raises the question of whether China has gained export market share and foreign investment at the expense of the rest of Asia? Some critics even link the 1997/1998 Asian financial crisis to China's devaluation of the renminbi (RMB) in 1994 and her flooding of the world market with cheap products in the subsequent years. They claim that these Chinese economic strategies crowded out Southeast Asian exports, thus worsening Southeast Asia's current account deficits and eventually pushing their currencies over the cliff.

However, such views are myopic. They ignore the structural and policy faults of the inefficient use of domestic savings and foreign capital inflow, bad banking systems, and erroneous macroeconomic policies in Asian economies before the crisis. Crucially, on the currency, trade and foreign investment fronts, there is no evidence that China has gained at Southeast Asia's expense, despite the competitive stress that China has inflicted in the region. But it is unfortunate that many Asian government and corporate leaders have exploited the "Chinese thief" conspiracy to avoid painful structural reforms.

No Chinese Thief

Let us look at the currency issue first. During the 1980s and early 1990s, China was making a transition towards a more market-oriented system, with her economy emerging as a crucial player in the regional and global markets. The Mainland started to liberalise its foreign exchange regime in the early 1990s to accommodate the rising importance of international trade and increasing foreign exchange transactions volume. It set up a swap market, which ran in parallel to the central bank's foreign exchange window, for foreign exchange transactions.

China thus had a dichotomised foreign exchange market before 1994. The swap foreign exchange market traded the renminbi (RMB) according to supply and demand conditions and was free from price fixing by the government. But the central bank's foreign exchange window traded the RMB at a fixed official exchange rate of 5.8 RMB per US dollar, irrespective of market forces. There were two characteristics in this set up. First, on paper, most of the foreign trade transactions were carried out using the official exchange rate. The portion of foreign trade using the swap rate was unknown, as there was no central record of these transactions. Second, despite differences between the swap and official exchange rates, strict capital controls had eliminated arbitrage between the two markets. This means that even if the official rate was lower than the swap rate, one was unable to buy from the official market and sell into the swap market to make a profit. The same restriction applies when the official rate was higher as no arbitrage trades of buying from the cheaper swap market and selling into the official market was possible.

This dichotomised foreign exchange market is a unique example of China's experimental system with a hybrid of market forces working within a planned economic framework. However, such a hybrid market structure is a huge economic distortion within the system, as the price of the local currency, that is the exchange rate, cannot adjust freely to changing market forces. The resultant adjustment problems affect external competitiveness. This can be seen in the economic problems that China experienced in the early 1990s when her exchange rate was pegged to the US dollar and her inflation rate rose consistently and significantly higher than that of her Asian neighbours and the US.

Higher inflation acts to erode export competitiveness because it makes local production cost dearer than overseas. In other words, higher inflation is equivalent to a rise in the exchange rate in real purchasing power terms with negative implications on export competitiveness. Given China's higher inflation, the Chinese authorities then faced a policy dilemma. They could devalue the RMB's official nominal exchange rate to offset the domestic inflation disadvantage, thus keeping real exchange rate competitiveness. Or they could keep the nominal RMB exchange rate at the official rate, thus accepting the rise in the real exchange rate and hurting Chinese exports.

The large inflation differential between China and her major trading partners, with Chinese inflation amounting to over 20 percentage points higher in 1995 and 1996, also opened up a large gap between the nominal exchange rates in the swap and official markets. This was because the nominal swap exchange rate had depreciated in response to higher inflation eroding export competitiveness, while the official rate was fixed. Thus, in the absence of any official currency devaluation, China's high inflation was inflicting damage in the export sector. The enlarging gap between the swap and official nominal exchange rates was forcing Beijing to rethink its fixed exchange rate policy: to devalue or not to devalue? Finally, the authorities decided on 1 January 1994 to unify the RMB official rate with the swap rate. At that time, the swap rate was trading at 8.7 RMB per US dollar. Thus, the exchange rate unification meant a near 50% devaluation of the official rate (from 5.8 RMB per USD to 8.7 RMB), which critics used as evidence of China's devaluation undercutting Southeast Asia's export competitiveness.

For example, the Financial Times editorial page argued on 17 September 1997 that "a large part of China's recent export success reflects the devaluation that occurred in January 1994"; that China continued to pursue "a cheap currency policy"; and that this was "one of the factors provoking the crisis in Southeast Asia". The Economist magazine also argued on 22 November 1997 that the Chinese devaluation of 1994 created an export boom that "may have laid the ground for some of Southeast Asia's woes".

However, these views missed some crucial economic truths. First, nominal currency depreciation does not necessarily give exports a boost because, as noted above, high domestic inflation (which raises local production costs) could negate the competitive gains from nominal exchange rate depreciation. This was indeed what happened to China after the 1994 devaluation. China's higher inflation rate, which rose to 24% in 1996, relative to her major trading partners, had offset the Mainland's effective exchange rate depreciation, giving Chinese exporters no competitive edges.

Second, focusing on the RMB/USD exchange rate is wrong because most Chinese exports do not compete with US exports in third markets, nor do they even compete with onshore local US industries. China does not export only to the US. Europe and Asia are also important markets in aggregate terms for China. All this means that the RMB/USD exchange rate is only one foreign exchange rate that affects China's competitiveness. There are other foreign exchange rates vis-à-vis Europe and Asia that should be taken into account when looking at China's overall competitiveness.

For example, if the RMB devalues against the USD, but its exchange rate rises against the European and Asian economies, the overall Chinese competitiveness could drop, not rise! In other words, if the rise in Chinese exports to the US, due to the devaluation of the RMB against the US dollar, is offset by the fall in exports to Europe and Asia, due to the rise of the RMB against European and Asian currencies, China will not gain any external competitiveness by devaluation. The ultimate impact on Chinese exports of the RMB devaluation against the US dollar depends on whether there is an offsetting appreciation of the RMB against other currencies.

Since both the local inflation rate and the weight of the trading partner matter, the relevant measure of export competitiveness should be China's inflation-adjusted, trade-weighted exchange rate, or the so-called real effective exchange rate, against her major trading partners. As higher inflation leads to higher domestic production cost, it raises the real effective exchange rate, thus hurting competitiveness. By this measure, the RMB's real effective exchange rate had actually risen by 20% between 1995 and 1998 because of China's significantly higher inflation rate relative to her trading partners. The real effective exchange rate appreciation also underscored the fact that the negative impact of high domestic inflation had more than offset the positive impact of nominal devaluation on China's exports. How could then one argue that the RMB's nominal devaluation against the US dollar boosted China's exports at the expense of other Asian exporters?

Lastly, and perhaps most crucially, most analyses implicitly assume that all foreign trade was transacted at the official exchange rate. However, research evidence gathered by influential and well-regarded institutions shows that prior to the unification of the official and swap exchange rates in 1994, a considerable amount of transactions occurred at the swap rate. For example, the International Monetary Fund (IMF) research in 1994 and 1996 showed that, prior to the exchange rate unification in 1994, only about 20% of foreign trade was transacted at the official exchange rate while the rest was done through the swap market rate.

This distinction is crucial because the swap rate was driven by market forces and not controlled by the government. Thus, China's high inflation had forced the real effective exchange rate in the swap market to appreciate sharply by about 20%, according to data from the Institute of International Finance. But in the official market, the 50% nominal devaluation of the official exchange rate on January 1994 had more than offset this real appreciation effect. This means that the relative amount of foreign trade transactions done at the official and swap markets could have considerable different implications on China's exchange rate competitiveness and, hence, the argument of whether China's devaluation in 1994 had triggered the Asian crisis three years later.

On one hand, if all transactions were done through the official rate, then the nominal devaluation, which overwhelmed the RMB's real appreciation, would have undercut the export competitiveness of Southeast Asia. This would support the critics' claims that the RMB devaluation was a culprit for the regional crisis. On the other hand, if all transactions were done at the swap rate, its sharp real effective exchange rate appreciation would have eroded China's competitiveness, dispelling the critics' claims. Thus, evidence from the IMF studies that 80% of China's foreign trade was done at the swap rate refutes the argument that China's nominal devaluation had undercut Southeast Asian exports and pushed their currencies over the cliff.

One may argue that the IMF calculation might be too extreme. This is because many of foreign trade businesses in the 1980s and early 1990s were done through state-controlled companies in China. Thus, the official foreign exchange market must have accounted for a bigger share of transactions than the IMF's estimation. Nevertheless, the point is that there is no clear-cut evidence for arguing that the RMB devaluation in 1994 was a decisive blow to Asia's economic woes. In a nutshell, China has emerged as a major competitor to many of Southeast Asian exports, and this may have put downward pressure on tradable goods prices in the regional markets.

Let us turn to the trade issue. Each year, Asia sells about half of its total exports to the OECD industrial countries, which in aggregate is the largest export market for emerging Asia. China has become an important force in global trade since the 1980s, with her exports, mostly manufactured goods, to OECD economies rising steadily. For instance, Chinese statistics show that the share in goods and services sold to OECD economies had more than doubled within a decade, from 8.5% of China's total exports in 1990 to 20% in 2000.

If China had displaced Southeast Asian exports, we should have seen the region's export share in the OECD markets decline. This would be especially true for the ASEAN4 – Indonesia, Malaysia, the Philippines and Thailand – because they compete closely with China in low-value exports. But this was not the case. Instead, the ASEAN4's exports to OECD countries had also increased in the 1990s. It was the four Newly Industrialised Economies (NIE4) of Hong Kong, South Korea, Taiwan, and Singapore who had seen a drop in their exports to the OECD area during the period.

In fact, the increase in China's export market share in the OECD reflects a subtle shift in trade distribution among Asian exporters, but not "Chinese theft" of Asia's market share. This shift in turn reflects a changing pattern of foreign direct investment flows into Asia, as the production of labour-intensive manufacturing goods moves to China and other low-cost economies, including the ASEAN4, from the high cost NIE4. Meanwhile, in the NIE4 economies, high-tech and high value-added production has replaced the traditional manufacturing exports.

Production and trade data from China's Trade Ministry show that in the 1980s and 1990s, a large portion of China's exports to OECD countries were produced by firms either wholly- or majority-owned by foreign companies, mostly from Hong Kong and Taiwan. This is consistent with the economic development in Hong Kong and Taiwan since the 1980s, when their manufacturing sectors migrated to China in search for a low-cost production base. Hence, goods that were once produced in Hong Kong and Taiwan are being produced in and exported from the Mainland, causing a rise in China's exports and a fall in Hong Kong's and Taiwan's exports.

Aggregate export data also do not support the "Chinese theft" theory. If China had stolen Southeast Asian exports, export data should have shown a rise in China's export growth at the expense of Southeast Asia's. But in fact, China's export growth has tracked closely the ups and downs of Southeast Asia's export growth over the past 20 years. This evidence is seen in Figure 4.1, which argues clearly against the view that Chinese exports have displaced Asian exports.

Figure 4.1   Chinese Exports Tracking Asia's

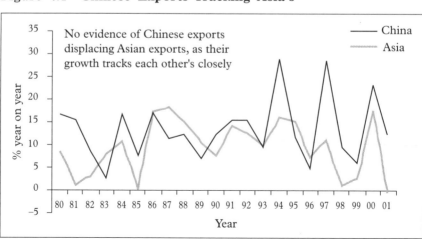

Skeptics have also charged that excess capacity and high inventory, especially in the first half of the 1990s, must have prompted China to dump cheap apparel and textile products in the global market. This, in turn, must have hurt Southeast Asia's textile exports to the US. Since the US is Asia's largest export market for apparel and textile products, the alleged Chinese dumping must have caused a major disruption to the region's economic lifeline. This should have eroded Southeast Asia's external balances badly, so goes the argument, causing the region's current account deficit to explode, depleting its foreign exchange reserves, and eventually triggering the 1997/1998 Asian financial crisis.

This argument does not sit well with the facts either. During the two years before the 1997/1998 regional crisis, China saw a 2% fall in textile export value and an 8% decline in textile export volume to the US. But in the same period, the textile export value of all ASEAN4 economies rose and the export volume also rose for three of these economies, except Malaysia. Overall, Asia, including China, the NIE4, and the ASEAN4, has been losing textile export market share in the US in recent years. This is because the US government has altered its import quota allocations to favour the western hemisphere at the expense of Asia.

All this evidence shows that the rise of China's export power did not cause Southeast Asia's economic problems. They were a result of bad domestic economic policies and crony capitalism breeding economic bubbles across the region. When the economic bubbles burst, the structural faults of excessive foreign borrowing and balance sheet mismatch in the local banking systems were quickly exposed. Foreign investor confidence was shattered when they saw these problems together with Asia's bulging current account deficits. Fear and pessimism replaced greed and hype, prompting them to withdraw *en masse* from Asia and causing a domino effect on the region's financial markets.

Rather, the perceived competitive threat of China has brought benefits to some Asian economies by prompting them to change. South Korea and Taiwan provide notable examples of adaptive survivors that contrast sharply with Southeast Asia's failure to change. Cross-border experience of their companies has illustrated how firms that learn to straddle China's borders are gaining a competitive edge in the global economy. For example, the South Korean Cheil Industries, a unit of the conglomerate Samsung Corporation, makes some of the world's finest fabrics in China. Knowing that production cost is high at home, Cheil is producing high value-added, high-end luxury goods for China's growing market of affluence. To tackle the cost problem, it has moved manufacturing to low-cost China and brought Chinese workers to operate some of its high-tech plants at home. Crucially, Cheil has transformed itself from a financially strapped company in the late 1990s into the most competitive global player in its industry by 2000. All this owes to its flexibility and willingness to change, and its vision to tap the Chinese market by using cheap Chinese resources.

Taiwan businesses have also invested as much as US$100 billion across the Taiwan Strait since the 1980s, and China has become the island's biggest export market in Asia (see Chapter 7 for more discussions on Taiwan's economic migration to China). Cross-strait business cooperation has become a way of economic survival for the Taiwanese. For example, in a landmark deal in early 2002, consumer appliance makers Sampo Group of Taiwan and Haier Group of China formed a strategic alliance valued at more than US$300 million to make and sell each other's refrigerators, telecommunications equipment, and computer peripherals both in their home and global markets. Even Singapore is trying to catch up with these Northeast Asian neighbours. In July 2002, the Government of Singapore Investment Corporation (GSIC) announced its largest China investment to date, paying US$42 million for a Shanghai site for commercial development.

There is no evidence that China has stolen Asia's lunch. Meanwhile, the Chinese economic stress on Asia has brought out the best structural efforts of some Asian economies. It should be increasingly apparent that in the new economic paradigm, only those who are willing to change will survive. Those who are complacent and lag behind in the new competitive game will risk being stuck in a prolonged economic quagmire.

What's Right and What's Wrong?

The argument that China has been gaining foreign investment at the expense of the rest of Asia is also flawed. While China is likely to continue to get the bulk of foreign investment inflow, globalisation driven by relative production strengths, or comparative advantage, of regional economies means that foreign investment into Asia is a net sum game (see Chapter 3). Indeed, evidence shows that foreign direct investment (FDI) inflows to Asia have risen along with inflows to China. FDI inflows to China averaged US$32 billion a year in the first half of the 1990s, jumping by 45% to an annual average of US$60 billion in the second half of the decade. Meanwhile, FDI flows to the rest of Asia averaged US$15 billion a year between 1991 and 1995, jumping by 54% to an annual average of US$33 billion between 1996 and 2000. The strong complementarity is illustrated in Figure 4.2. But the Chinese investment magnet begs the question of why does China attract most of the FDI inflows, despite her economic woes, many of which are similar to Japan's?

The Chinese investment magnet seems to suggest that China might have done something right that Japan did not do in the 1990s. This view stands out prominently because, even though

Figure 4.2 Foreign Direct Investment Inflows to China and the Rest of Asia

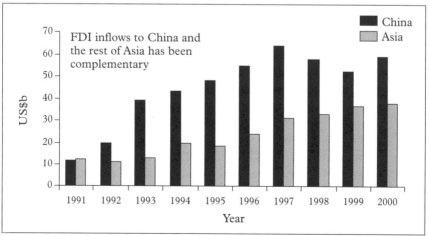

both are at different economic development stages, China and Japan have shared many common economic problems since the 1990s. They include excessive investment (which is reflective of excessive domestic savings and over-capacity), price deflation, and corporate and financial inefficiencies. These common woes have created similar macroeconomic problems in the two economies, such as capital misallocation, poor profit margins, deflation, and bankrupted financial systems. The latter is a particularly serious problem, as it has led to the so-called financial disintermediation. This is a distortion in the banking system where banks are impaired by mountains of bad debts. They are thus unable to function properly as a capital allocation mechanism, the essence of financial intermediation. Companies are being starved of credit or have to bypass banks to raise funds directly from the capital markets. The broken banking system is also a major culprit for stranding the Japanese economy in the doldrums since the early 1990s.

Yet, evidence shows that China might have pursued a better reform-growth policy mix than Japan and many other Asian economies in dealing with these woes. Relative to most of her Asian neighbours, China is the notable economy that has delivered steady, albeit slow, reform progress since the Asian crisis. The creative destruction process is seen in the shrinkage of China's inefficient state sector where the Chinese government destroys old and inefficient industries and replaces them with new and efficient ones. Since the Asian crisis, the number of state-owned enterprises (SOEs) has declined steadily from almost 40% of total enterprises in the economy to less than 30% in 2002. Meanwhile, the SOEs' aggregate asset value has fallen from 70% of the total corporate asset value in the economy to less than 60% during the same period. In terms of production, Chinese state companies now produce less than 25% of total industrial output, down from over 80% in the early 1980s.

There are also signs for the growing role of market forces and increased competition driving China's economic restructuring. Notably, average Chinese tariffs have fallen from 43% to about 15% from 1997 to 2002, and they will continue to fall in the coming years. As lower tariffs have increased competition, productivity has also risen, with output per worker rising by an average of 5% a year since 1999 compared to less than 1% before that. Foreign firms with access to western technology, machinery, and management have also prompted significant competition in the domestic economy. They produce 20% of all manufactured goods. That is similar to foreign firms' production share of manufactured goods in the US, where there are few restrictions on foreign ownership. Foreign firms' output share in China will continue to grow, as the country opens up further, leading to more competition and efficiency gains for the local industries.

More competition has also empowered Chinese consumers to have greater choice. All this has lessened the demand-supply mismatch problem in the economy. Under the old output quota system, Chinese firms only focused on meeting the official production quotas but not customer demand. Hence, they produced wasteful goods that the market did not want. But market liberalisation and increased profit incentives, as the private sector grows, have prompted firms to focus on output that meets market demand and on products that can deliver profits. Overall growth quality has thus improved.

Meanwhile, unemployment has soared as closure of the SOEs releases millions of surplus workers a year. China's true unemployment rate is estimated by private sector analysts at close to 10% of the labour force, compared to the official 3%. Employment in the state sector fell by 36 million, almost a third of the total, between 1999 and 2002. Rising bankruptcies and unemployment are clear signs that China is absorbing a substantial portion of the costs of adjusting to increasing competition in the domestic market. Many SOEs have been privatised and the non-state sector has become an important source of new jobs. As a result, SOEs' employment share in the economy has dropped precipitately since the regional crisis while the share and growth of private sector employment has risen sharply. While there is more economic pain to come as the reform process continues, there is a good prospect of the burgeoning private sector creating jobs to absorb workers laid off by the SOEs.

Wasteful inventory accumulation is down sharply, no longer reflecting the old priority of boosting growth in output and employment regardless of the impact on companies' bottom lines. After peaking at double-digit growth rates in the mid-1990s, China's inventory growth has been declining after the Asian crisis. Chinese companies have been cutting back on inventory accumulation since 1999 such that the corporate sector's inventory growth rate has turned negative. While a lot more restructuring needs to be done in rectifying China's industrial inefficiency, the fact that profitability in the shrunken state sector has recovered since the late 1990s, reversing a 20-year slide, is a sign the Chinese authorities have done something right.

On the other hand, Tokyo has been pouring money into a system that continues to resist change. Japan has had numerous prime ministers since the burst of her economic bubble in the early 1990s, with each new government promising reform, but only failed to deliver. The reform-minded Prime Minister Junichiro Koizumi, elected in mid-2001, had once raised investors' hope for reform. He came into office with slogans like "I am ready to crush the Liberal Democratic Party (LDP)", "Koizumi reform", and "a declaration of war against the forces of resistance". These penetrated deeply into the minds of millions of Japanese. They became his fervent followers, as seen in Koizumi's initially incredibly high approval ratings in opinion polls. But the enthusiasm died only months after he was installed because a complex and contentious old guard network had hampered his initiatives and made any reform effort difficult even under favourable economic conditions. Many realised that "Koizumi reform" was a vague concept without focus on specific issues. They became aware that his slogans "to breakup the LDP" and "the battle against reform resistance" were merely a stage show and no real battles were waged (see Chapters 5 and 8 for more discussions on Japan's reform failure).

Meanwhile, Japan's low unemployment rate also mirrors her reform inertia. The average 3% unemployment rate in the past ten years has been quite low by the developed world's standards and it should be consistent with a booming economy. But yet Japan's GDP growth averaged only 1.6% a year since the early 1990s! This combination of low unemployment and stagnant growth underscores the Japanese malaise of economic wastage in the form of a resistance to change combined with expansionary fiscal and monetary policies to misallocate resources to keep unemployment artificially low. Such an outdated policy approach stands in stark contrast to the changing Chinese attitude of throwing away the old system of producing for production's sake.

Finally, Japan's resistance to change can be seen in her production pattern. Despite her mature economy and technological advancement, Japan still produces many low value-added products, such as glasses, textiles, and shoes, which compete with China. This is incompatible with the law of comparative advantage, which argues that each country should focus on producing goods that has the lowest relative costs. Thus, when labour and other business costs rise in a mature economy like Japan, it should shed low value-added production and focus on high value-added output to make up for the cost disadvantage.

Japan has instead resorted to protectionism to sustain her sunset industries. The rise in Japan's protectionism against Chinese imports, notably after the Asian crisis, reflects her fears about China's competitive threat and her unwillingness to forgo the old economic system. Since the burst of her economic bubble, Japan has remained complacent about economic restructuring. The resultant loss of competitive power has manifested itself in a record trade deficit with China. The deficit had grown almost seven-fold from 430 billion yen (or US$3.6 billion) a year in 1990 to 2.92 trillion yen (US$24.3 billion) in 2001. This stunning trend is worrying, as it is accelerating exponentially as Chinese goods are climbing up the value-added ladder fast.

Walking a Fine Line

Hence, there lies a big difference in attitude towards change and reform between China and Japan. Japan has been in denial for years. She has been using single-handed economic expansionary policy to sustain growth. Whenever new shoots of economic growth emerge, the Japanese government has used them as excuses to put off tough reform choices. But China has so far been proactive in tackling her structural woes within her economic and political constraints by pursuing a two-prong approach that combines economic reforms with macro expansionary policies to boost growth. Knowing the potential short-term negative impact of structural reforms on growth, China has opted for a decisive fiscal expansion program to sustain growth. In addition to public spending, Beijing has also resorted to giving pay hikes to civil servants to boost consumption and large bond issuance to domestic banks to boost lending.

The bond issuance measure aims at lessening the damage of financial disintermediation in the economy. Due to their broken balance sheets, Chinese banks have been unable and unwilling to lend, trapping a large pool of idle funds in the banking system. By selling bonds to banks, Beijing collects the idle funds in terms of sale proceeds and puts them into investment. This way, the government is able to redirect idle savings in banks to investment via the bond market. Beijing has also implemented the so-called "holiday economics" by extending the three major holiday periods – the Lunar New Year, Labour Day, and National Day – from a few days to two weeks each, coupling with pay hikes to civil servants and factory workers to encourage consumer spending.

In contrast, Japan's policy makers seem to have lost their reform-growth balance. They wrongly kept interest rates high in the early 1990s when the asset bubble was bursting. This had worsened deflation and destroyed the macroeconomic environment for reform. The Japanese authorities also prematurely raised the consumption tax in 1999, and then interest rates in 2000, suffocating the fragile economy. A poor economy has in turn hampered Japan's reform initiatives. The Japanese reform programmes seem to have been stuck in a Catch-22 situation inflicted by the government – reforms are damned when the economy is poor; they are also damned when the economy is good!

But China's massive fiscal expansion has raised doubts about the policy's sustainability, as her fiscal deficit has been widening swiftly. Indeed, Beijing's finances will become a problem in the longer term if left unattended. Nevertheless, they are not a concern in the short term because the huge amount of household savings (US$800 billion and growing) idling in the banking system will be sufficient to fund fiscal needs. Going forward, Beijing needs to show more initiatives in halting the worsening fiscal and public debt positions. China's fiscal reforms should take a two-prong approach to raise revenue intake and cut wasteful spending as part of the overall structural reform programme to sustain public confidence. Beijing should focus on revenue-raising measures, such as standardising local and foreign corporate taxes, and to widen the tax net and close tax loopholes, as well as cuts on unnecessary spending during normal economic times.

On the financial side, the heart of Asia's structural problems, both China and Japan are in dire straits. But Beijing has taken a bolder move than Tokyo to deal with her banking problems. The Chinese government has set up asset management companies to take bad debt off bank balance sheets, ordered Chinese banks to write off at least 2% of bad debt each year, and injected massive funds to improve the capital base of the banking sector. The Japanese government has also set up an asset management company to deal with bank bad debts. However, it has the wrong initiatives, although the asset management vehicle is based on the right concept (see Chapter 5). It has also injected massive amounts of funds into the banking system. But without enforcing structural changes, pure cash injection has failed to create final demand. This is because bank balance sheets remain burdened by bad loans, creating a disincentive to lend. Heavy debt load and worsening credit risk in the Japanese corporate sector has also curbed borrowing power, while Chinese corporates have shown a recovery in profitability in recent years.

Thus, despite a loose monetary policy, the Japanese authorities have failed to create credit growth. An economy without credit growth is just like a human body with a failing heart. No matter how much food is fed, there is no strength if there is insufficient blood pumped through the system. Such a failing body is exactly what Japan has been stuck with for over a decade for failing to bite the reform bullet. Since there is no credit growth, no matter how much money the Japanese authorities have pumped into the banking system, the expected positive economic impact has never materialised.

There is strong evidence showing the ineffectiveness of Japan's economic bailout without structural reforms. Just look at the ratio of credit-to-money growth. When increasing money supply does not generate any credit growth, the ratio will fall as the numerator remains stagnant while the denominator expands. The writing is on the wall, as Figure 4.3 shows, that Japan's credit-to-money growth ratio has declined steadily throughout the 1990s and into the 21st century. In the mid-1990s, for example, every 1% of money supply growth generated about 0.74% of bank credit growth. But bank credit has been contracting since the Asian crisis under the weight of Japan's structural problems and poor economy. By 2001, every 1% of monetary growth was met by 1.3% decline in bank loans. This not only underscores the weak-heart-sick-body analogy above, it also highlights the risk of a downward spiral in economic growth because the rise in money supply has not been able to halt the reduction in credit growth. On the other hand, China's ratio has remained stable during the period, suggesting that Chinese monetary expansion effort had been met by rising bank credit growth. The lack of credit is a major reason why Japan's economy has remained stagnant for so long while China's economy has managed to pull through the Asian crisis and the global economic slowdown in 2001 and 2002.

Figure 4.3   Gap between Money and Loan Growth

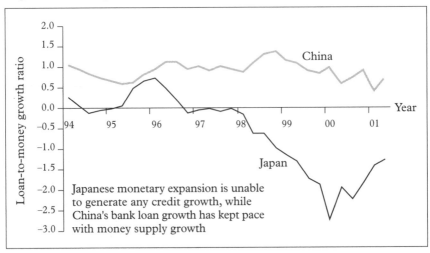

The Chinese Magnet and Southeast Asia

There is really no secret behind the Chinese magnet for FDI. Despite all her economic problems, China has been popular among foreign investors because of her positive reform attitude and macroeconomic policy mix to facilitate structural changes. By contrast, Japan has been stuck with inertia to preserve vested interests of the existing system by throwing good money after bad. By the same token, the lack of aggressive reforms and the existence of economic policy imbalance in Southeast Asia have raised the risk of the region, except Singapore, being marginalised as a FDI destination in the coming years.

Nevertheless, even China has to understand that attracting FDI inflows, as a policy stance, should be of secondary importance to those structural reforms that seek to improve resource allocation in the economy. These microeconomic and institutional reforms should include removing the political, regulatory, and financial constraints on China's private sector. The essence of these changes is to intensify creative destruction to clean up the corporate sector. Creative destruction is the process where old and inefficient production facilities are being destroyed, via bankruptcies, closures, and/or restructuring, while new and more efficient output facilities are being installed. China's new membership in the WTO will facilitate this process, as the rules and requirements of the trade body will act as an external discipline on pushing Chinese economic reforms. The key to success is to sustain the resultant reform momentum.

The FDI inflow outlook need not be dim for Southeast Asia. Subtly, Southeast Asia is not competing with China for foreign capital. It is facing a challenge of reinventing itself to attract foreign investment! This is because China's eventual economic maturity will eat into her returns on investment over the long term, reducing her relative attractiveness for foreign investment inflow. In addition, there is a growing pool of global capital looking for a home in high-return markets, including Asia. This point suggests that local factors in individual economies would play an important role in attracting capital inflow.

Thailand is a case in point. Fifteen years after Japan Inc.

began uprooting factories at home and relocating them to cheaper Southeast Asia, a new relocation wave is underway. The main investment destination this time is Thailand. Though China is the single largest destination for foreign direct investment within Asia in most of the 1990s, many Japanese firms are also putting an increasing amount of their money in Thailand as a way of hedging their bets in China. In the first half of 2002, according to data from JETRO (an agency that monitors investment activities of Japanese multinational companies), Japanese direct investment in Thailand was up more than 65% year-on-year, following a trend of double-digit growth since 2000.

The Japanese are attracted by Thailand's local competitive factors. JETRO found that Thailand outranked China in a number of investment criteria, including infrastructure, technical skills, quality of engineers, and better (than China) transparency of investment-related law. On the other hand, China outranked Thailand in production costs and market potential. In 2002, a JETRO survey of Japanese multinationals also ranked Thailand as the third-most attractive investment destination for future Japanese overseas investment, trailing after China and the US. Thailand's growing allure is most evident in the auto industry. In 2002, major Japanese motor companies, including Isuzu Motors Ltd., Toyota Motor Corp., Honda Motor Co., and Mitsubishi Motors Corp. (in conjunction with DaimlerChrysler AG), all launched new production plants or announced plans to expand operations in Thailand.

Thailand's success in courting Japanese investment is also, in part, an indirect result of China's popularity among foreign investors. This, in turn, serves to vindicate the point that China's prosperity offers opportunities for the rest of Asia. JETRO's study of Japanese multinationals found that 30% of Japanese investment since 2000 in Thailand was done as a hedge against their heavy investment in the Middle Kingdom – the "don't put all your eggs in one basket" thinking prevails. Japanese investors are concerned about the lack of intellectual property protection in China. In particular, Japanese motorcycle manufacturers operating in China alleged certain Chinese companies were pirating their product designs and exporting similar vehicles at cut-rate prices. The Thai authorities have been quick to exploit this problem in China and highlight the difference in intellectual property rights protection between the Middle and Thai Kingdoms. Notably, in mid-2002, the Thai government launched a high-profile intellectual property protection fair, using bulldozers to crush counterfeit Japanese wares.

Thailand's experience shows clearly the point that local factors are crucial for competing for foreign investment with China, despite the Chinese investment magnet. There is no reason to believe foreign capital will only and always flow into China. To understand how economic dynamics will eventually erode China's investment returns, consider the simple business logic of a firm hiring a worker. A firm will continue to hire if the worker continues to produce goods that generate a value higher than the cost of hiring. In other words, a firm will continue to hire if the marginal value of output is larger than the marginal cost of hiring the worker. Conversely, if the marginal value is lower than the marginal cost, the firm will cut back. Thus, equilibrium exists only when the marginal value equals the marginal cost.

Putting this into perspective, foreign investors will continue to invest in China at the expense of Southeast Asia only when Chinese workers consistently work for, and thus get paid, less than the marginal value of their output. It is only under this circumstance that there would be a fat margin left behind for foreign investors, attracting more and more foreign capital to the Middle Kingdom and starving others of capital. But this is implausible in the long term! As China continues to grow, diminishing returns will set in, wages and other costs will rise, and the local business environment will become increasingly competitive. All this will erode the profit margin for foreign investors.

Some may wonder if China's massive population would keep Chinese labour cost cheap, especially when economic liberalisation leads to higher labour mobility between regions. This is possible but only partly, and that is why China is unlikely to see a significant rise in the general wage level in the short- to medium-term. However, in the longer term, as labour mobility increases, the workers from various parts of the country will become more integrated into urban economies. They will behave the same way as their urban counterparts and push for better remuneration, thus raising overall business costs.

It is myopic to opine that China would be able to combine cheap labour with technology to become super-competitive and drain capital flow from Asia. When the Chinese economy continues to grow towards its capacity constraint, resources will become scarce and production costs will rise. It will thus follow the same fate of diminishing returns as in any other economy. Just look at the experience of South Korea, where wages have risen from less than one-tenth to more than two-fifths of American levels since the 1990s. And there is no evidence that South Korea received the lion's share of foreign investment inflow in Asia during the 1990s when South Korean wages were still low. The point is that every nation has a comparative advantage due to their endowment differences in areas such as education, infrastructure, labour market, and technology. Southeast Asian economies must also have their own comparative advantages that will attract foreign capital inflow.

Then there is the issue of global supply of capital. Since there is a growing pie of global capital looking for investment homes in Asia, local factors in each country are crucial in determining the share of foreign capital it will attract. The developed world's baby-boomers want to maximise their investment returns, and hence the size of their pension, before retirement. But they do not earn sustained high returns on their savings by investing in mature markets like those in their home countries. There is thus a big need to diversify into emerging markets, including those in Asia, where returns on investment are higher due to faster growth potentials.

Therefore, despite a lot of foreign capital flowing to China, there is still ample available for the rest of Asia. That is why Southeast Asia does not just face a Chinese competition in attracting foreign capital. More fundamentally, it faces an internal challenge of reinventing itself to attract foreign investment. If Southeast Asia could pursue appropriate economic policies to nurture a stable, transparent, and fair institutional and regulatory base for foreign businesses, capital will flow in even if it is also going to China.

In a nutshell, while China may continue to get the bulk of foreign investment inflow, the trend of global outsourcing driven by specialisation and comparative advantage of different economies means that investment opportunities are not restricted to China. Whether it is South Korea's semiconductor makers, Taiwan's chip designers, Singapore's biotech companies, or Thailand's vehicle-component manufacturers, each economy has its production edge. Structural reforms to rebuild an economy's infrastructure software, such as labour skills, corporate governance, transparency, and a reliable legal and institutional framework, and hardware, such as transport links, fixed capital, and environmental protection, are key to attract foreign capital. Strong foreign capital inflow to China will also benefit other Asian economies via intra-regional demand for goods and services stemming from the different competitive edges of different economies. And rising intra-regional economic links should act as a cushion for Asia to take the challenges posted by China as it enters the new economic paradigm.

Chapter 5

Changing Fortunes Between the Yen and the Renminbi

The Asian crisis has reduced Japan's influence and raised China's impact sharply on Asia's economies and markets. Indeed, the 1997/1998 regional crisis has highlighted the helplessness of Japan to act as an economic engine to salvage the region from the financial chaos. On the other hand, it is a watershed that marks the beginning of China's role in shaping Asia's post-crisis economic transformation. Japan was more adversely affected by the regional crisis not only because she had stronger economic ties with Southeast Asia, but also because the crisis occurred at a time when the Japanese economy was in its deepest recession since the Second World War. As a result, the Japanese yen exchange rate, and its influence on Asia's economic well-being, has fallen since the elapse of the Asian crisis.

On the other hand, the closed nature of the Chinese economy and Beijing's tight capital controls on international fund flows has helped minimise the negative impact of the Asian crisis on the Middle Kingdom. Hence, the Chinese renminbi (RMB) has remained stable, despite rounds of currency devaluation in Asia since 1997. China's commitment not to devalue the RMB has also enhanced her credibility and bargaining power in the global economic and political arenas. Arguably, China gains largely at the expense of Japan. With declining Japanese economic influence in Asia and rising Chinese economic clout (see Chapters 3 and 4), the RMB will become more crucial than the Japanese yen in affecting Asia's economic stability, especially when China starts to overtake Japan as the region's economic powerhouse.

Japan's Fading Glory

Before the bursting of Japan's bubble economy in 1990, Asia used to rely heavily on Japan as a major foreign creditor and export market. Japanese bank loans accounted for 53% of all Asian foreign borrowing and Japanese foreign direct investment (FDI) accounted for 26% of all Asian FDI inflows in the 1980s and early 1990s. Meanwhile, Japan was Asia's largest export market within the region, buying more than 15% of all Asian exports during the same period. As a result, the Japanese currency used to have a significant influence on Asia's economic development, with its exchange rate movement affecting the region's livelihood both positively and negatively.

Take a weaker yen for example. On the positive side, a falling yen lowers the cost of imports from Japan for many Asian economies, which relies on Japan as a source of capital and intermediate goods. Lower import prices in turn translate into lower input prices and boost output and profits for the regional companies. A fall in the yen also reduces the debt-servicing burden for those Asian countries that have foreign borrowing denominated in yen. The bulk of Asia's yen-denominated debt is in the form of official development assistance (ODA) from the Japanese government to the less developed countries. Thus, the less developed Asian economies tend to benefit more from a weak yen through a larger decline in foreign debt burden than the more developed ones, which have less ODA loans.

Offsetting these positive effects of a weaker yen, however, are a decline in Asian (sans Japan) export competitiveness and a slowdown in capital inflow from Japan. A fall in the yen exchange rate reduces Japanese export prices, thus making Japanese exports cheaper relative to those of the rest of Asia. As a result, Asian exporters (excluding Japan) suffer deterioration in international competitiveness against the Japanese. One may wonder how much direct competition do Japan and the rest of Asia have, given the difference in their stages of economic development. Despite Japan's more advanced economic image, she still produces many low value-added products, such as glasses, textiles and shoes, which compete with many less developed economies, including China. This is clearly incompatible with the law of comparative advantage. The economic principle argues that developed economies should shed low value-added production and focus on high value-added output to make up for their cost disadvantage. The fact that Japan still sustains her sunset industries is strong evidence of the country's resistance to reform.

A weaker yen also tends to reduce Japanese foreign investment abroad because it makes acquiring overseas production facilities relatively expensive. The resultant decline in Japanese investment in Asia has the effect of dampening the region's economic growth. This is because less Japanese investment inflow reduces the demand for factors of production from Japanese investors. Such a reduction in demand sets off a negative chain effect on the local economy. For example, a cut in Toyota's investment in Thailand will reduce demand for Thai labour, glasses, steel, and other raw materials for car production. This will, in turn, cut the business for Toyota's suppliers in Thailand, reducing their demand for labour and other goods and services, thus setting off a chain of demand reduction.

In addition to the decline in direct investment, Japanese bank lending to Asia also tends to fall when the yen is weak. First, foreign exchange losses, due to a falling yen, discourage the Japanese incentive to lend overseas by reducing the return on the loans after exchange rate adjustment. Second, the lending drop is also due to the need to meet international capital adequacy requirements. The Bank for International Settlements (BIS), the central bank of central banks and an international banking watchdog, stipulates a minimum 8% capital/asset ratio for all international banks engaged in cross-border lending. That is, all banks must have capital amounting to 8% of their asset as a safety cushion for their business. A fall in the yen exchange rate automatically inflates the value of overseas loan assets of Japanese banks even though they did not increase lending. This reduces the capital/asset ratio by inflating its denominator. To comply with the BIS minimum capital rule, Japanese banks have to shrink their asset size by reduce lending, if they do not put in more capital.

The ultimate effect of a yen exchange rate movement on Asian economies depends on the relative magnitude of these positive and negative forces. During the yen's heyday, its impact was unevenly spread across the region because some countries would be hurt, while some others would benefit more, depending on their trade, investment and loan exposure to Japan.

Nevertheless, the yen's influence on Asia has faded steadily along with the decline in Japan's economic importance to Asia since the 1990s. The main reasons were two-fold. One was due to Japan's financial weakness after her economic bubble burst in the early 1990s, and the other was due to Asia's emergence as an export power in the global market. The former reduces Japan's ability to lend and invest abroad, while the latter reduces Asia's economic dependence of Asia on Japan. On the financial side, data from the Institute of International Finance (a think-tank for global banks, based in Washington D.C.) shows that the shares of Japanese bank loans and FDI in Asia's total foreign capital intake have fallen sharply since the 1990s. The share of bank loans fell from an average of 53% before the regional crisis to less than 25% in 2001, while the FDI share fell from a pre-crisis average of 26% to 11%. This decline occurred at a time when foreign, especially European, investment in Asia was surging. The rate of decline in Japanese capital flow to the rest of Asia has accelerated since the regional crisis, as mounting domestic banking woes have reduced Japanese risk appetite for Asian projects.

The fall in Asia's economic dependence on Japan is clearly seen in the robust Asian GDP growth rate in the decade before the Asian crisis. During that period, Asia (excluding Japan) grew at an average of 6% a year while Japan grew at a meager 1.6%. This growth divergence in fact mirrors a shift in the balance of foreign trade power between Asia and Japan. Since the 1990s, Asia's reliance on Japanese demand for Asian imports has been falling, while Japan's reliance on exports to Asian markets has been rising. This shift in the trade pattern is clearly evident from the regional trade trend shown in Figure 5.1.

In the late 1980s and early 1990s, Asian economies on average shipped about 15% of all their exports to Japan. But the

Figure 5.1   Change in Export Power

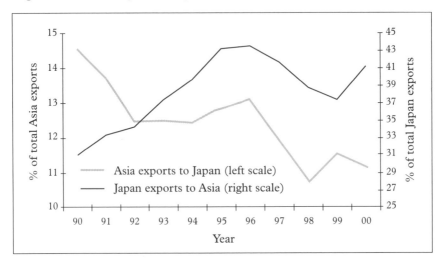

share dropped steadily to 11% by 2000, implying a fall in the importance of the Japanese market as an export destination for the rest of Asia. On the other hand, Japanese exports to the rest of Asia had risen from 30% of Japan's total exports in 1990 to over 40% in 2000. This suggests a steady rise in the importance of Asian markets for Japanese exporters. This trend has developed persistently despite disruption from the Asian crisis in 1997/1998. And it will continue because behind this switch in export power is the emergence of Asia (sans Japan) as a low-cost manufacturing base. This makes the region an export powerhouse penetrating the global market, thus reducing its reliance on Japan as the major market.

Driving Asia's export power is the significant "hollowing out" of Japanese industries. This process refers to the migration of Japanese industries from their home base to other Asian economies. Since the early 1990's, Japan and other developed countries started moving production to the emerging Asian economies in search for lower-cost bases. As most of these foreign facilities are export-oriented, this hollowing-out process has resulted in a sharp rise in exports by Asia to non-Japanese markets. Meanwhile, Japanese exports to emerging Asia have soared to feed the import needs of Japanese factory productions there.

Indeed, the Japanese hollowing-out process is a different form of outsourcing strategy to skirt high domestic cost structure. Instead of directly buying from cheaper suppliers in other Asian economies, which is what normal outsourcing does, the Japanese build their production facilities in Asia. This way, they can control business ownership, have access to cheaper production sources, and reap the earnings from the overseas operations. The steady rise in Japan's net national income (NNI) from abroad, which turned around dramatically and steadily from a deficit of 11 billion yen in 1980 to a surplus 6.3 trillion yen in 2000, reflects this Japanese hollowing-out process behind the change in trade flows. To see why, consider the definition of NNI. It is the difference between the investment income earned by Japanese firms from overseas and the income earned by foreign firms in Japan. In economics, it is simply the difference between gross national product (GNP) and gross domestic product (GDP). Given the amount of foreign investment at home, Japanese net foreign income rises as they invest and produce more overseas. Thus, the steady rise in Japan's NNI underscores the hollowing-out outsourcing strategy.

While being an economic survival strategy, the hollowing out of Japanese industry is also a strong signal of Japan's declining economic power. International trade and investment flows are the market mechanisms that allocate resources efficiently across national borders and raise real income in the countries involved. If hollowing out occurs, it reflects the existence of market and government failures that lead to distortions in pricing information and allocation of resources in the country. These distortions may include excessive exchange rate volatility, factors market failure, poor regulatory and fiscal systems, and incompatibility between macro and structural economic policies.

It is well known that Japan possessed many of these problems that intensified throughout the 1990s. The vested interests in Japan, notably the farmers, construction companies, and corporate dinosaurs, have only worsened them further. This is because these forces have significant influence over government policy and have blocked structural reforms all the way since Japan's asset bubble burst in the early 1990s. Thus, despite numerous economic bailout packages, which have amounted to over US$1 trillion in the 1990s, Tokyo has not been able to dig its economy out of the doldrums.

The Japanese Burden

Japan's inability to reform is the main reason why she will likely remain a lost economic power in Asia in the new economic paradigm. More importantly, the losts of Japan as a major demand source for global exporters, due to her economic weakness, will add deflationary pressures to the global system. This will in turn make Asia's economic transformation tougher than it would have been if Japan were a stronger economic force. Japan will eventually reform. And when she finally does, she will become an economic powerhouse again. Her IT revolution could prove even more powerful than other major economies. This is because all the resultant efficiency gains will be greater in Japan than many other developed economies. As Japan's inefficient industries reform, sustained economic growth of 3%, compared with an average of 1% in the 1990s, will be within reach. The bad news is that it will take more than a decade's bumpy journey for Japan to reach this steady state of growth. Why so pessimistic?

The root problem for Japan is denial. There is a strong inertia to change, despite over a decade of economic doldrums. The lack of reform has rendered government stabilisation policies to boost economic growth useless since the late 1980s, as the economy has been stuck in a quagmire. Japan's fiscal position has worsened so much that even the most conservative calculations suggest a rising risk of a downward economic spiral. The risk stems from Japan's huge debt burden and contingent liabilities in the banking and pension systems. Altogether, these problems add up to a gigantic demand for funds amounting to over three times Japan's total national output. In other words, if the Japanese economy were evaluated at present value terms, taking into account all these liabilities, it would be technically bankrupt. Monetary policy is also exhausted. Interest rates have been cut to zero since 2000 and they are likely to stay very low due to persistent deflation. This means that there would not be room for more rate cuts to boost growth. Printing money will do nothing to speed up Japan's restructuring process and prompt Japan's entrepreneurs to build more efficient companies than their credit-bubble-fed fathers did in the 1980s.

When there is a will, there is a way. But a will has been exactly what Japan lacks year after year. Without a will to restructure, there is no way she can pull herself out of the economic black hole. Japan's limited reform efforts have either run into the sands of resistance of the old guards, notably the ruling Liberal Democratic Party (LDP), or they have been met with indifference by her leaders. So deep-rooted are Japan's dysfunctions that even if she did everything right at once, it would take at least 5 years to get growth back on track. And Japan will not do everything right at once because the system is swamped by conflicting objectives of vested interests, which act as obstacles to change.

Notably, the very obstacles to growth serve as pillars of Japan's political system. Collusion, regulations, price controls, and soft loans to insolvent companies all serve as social safety nets that sustain the inefficiencies in the economy where only half the workforce is covered by unemployment insurance. The interest of those voters who would benefit from reform clashes with that of those who would be hurt by it. Without growth, these immense conflicts of interests will continue to mount and sabotage the leadership's decision-making process. Thus, each government action to plug the leaky dike just causes the leak to burst elsewhere.

For example, the Bank of Japan's zero interest rate policy used to keep borrowers and banks afloat have hurt the fixed-income earners, like life insurers, pension funds, and depositors. This, in turn, hurts the spending of millions of people. Meanwhile, firms' actions to cut staff and wages have caused millions of job losses and real (or inflation-adjusted) wage decline since 1997. But these casulties mean reduced spending. Profits slump as a result, setting off a negative domino effect on investment, employment, confidence, and demand. The fact that even a committed reformer, like Prime Minister Koizumi, has repeated reform errors of his predecessors shows the depth of Japan's dilemma. It also shows the strength of resistance within his LDP to any crackdown on the country's structural woes.

Japan's denial to change is clearly seen in the authorities' very effort to seize every sign of growth, which should provide an opportunity to make tough choices to bring economic efficiency and long-term growth, as an excuse to put off reforms. Two such high profile cases came in 2002 when Koizumi was trying to push through postal and banking reform measures, but failed in the end. Although Japan has been using excuses to skirt reform for years, these two excuses were hallmarks of reform resistance because they came at the time when hope was rising that Japan might finally put her act together under the reform-minded prime minister.

Koizumi has tried to break up the postal savings system ever since he was postal minister in the mid-1990s. The post office, which also acts as a bank taking household deposits, has 240 trillion yen (US$2 trillion) in assets and an extra 120 trillion yen in its life insurance system. It is in fact the world's largest bank. But the combination of being a giant government bureau and a deposit-taking institution has made the postal system a major economic distortion in the Japanese economy. This huge bureaucratic system undermines private-sector competitors by siphoning away household savings and rewarding them with only anemic investment return. It also funds a shadow budget that wastes money to its fullest extent on white elephant projects, such as smothering almost every hillside and watercourse in concrete, and building roads and bridges that only wildlife animals use. But this is not the only negative impact on the economy. There is a more subtle and serious indirect damage that stems from money sloshing around the system. In particular, the postal money keeps the old guards and reactionary vested interests in business, thus allowing them to continue to stymie structural reforms.

The resistance of these reactionary forces is so strong that it has stymied the long-overdue postal reform too. The postal reform bills that passed the Diet (Japan's parliament) in July 2002 were a travesty of Koizumi's reform ambitions. Not only did they fail to address the distortions caused by the savings and insurance systems, they even made a mockery of Koizumi's reform idea by focusing on mail delivery. And even there, reforms were unreal. Under the "reformed" system, competitors to the post office must set up a daunting minimum of 100,000 post boxes, while the legislation has barred any reduction in the number of state postal branches. Instead of making mail delivery more efficient, the reform bills have created a more costly and inefficient system!

The second notable excuse involved the personnel changes at the Financial Services Agency (FSA), which also happened in July 2002 when Koizumi's postal reform was watered down. The FSA is supposed to be in charge of cleaning up the banks' 150 trillion yen of bad debts. But instead of replacing its reactionary retired head, Shoji Mori, with a more reform-minded candidate, the agency replaced him with another LDP old guard, Hakuo Yanagisawa. And Yanagisawa is a superstar of Japan's reform inertia because the first thing he did when he took office in July 2002 was to deny that there was a banking crisis. He made no secret of his preference to prop up rotten banks by rigging the stock market to bolster bank capital, instead of weeding them out to purge the structural woes.

Yanagisawa had also pushed for mergers between small regional banks, but not for the restructuring reasons that banking reform would suggest. The purpose of bank mergers, as seen by the FSA, seems to be aimed at preventing bad banks from going under. Yanagisawa's initiatives differ little from the past when bank mergers led to no consolidation of the industry, as no branches were closed and redundant bank staff were not sacked. This means that Japan had again reneged on commitments to allow banks to sink or swim on the strength of their own lending practices, thus denying any opportunity to allow market forces to drive restructuring. Although Koizumi replaced Yanagisawa with Heigo Takenaka, who, like Koizumi, is also an ardent reformer, in October 2002, the damage was already done. Takenaka, being the Prime Minister's most trusted advisor and the most outspoken critic of the FSA's timid policies towards the banks, soon found himself stranded in thick reform resistance only days after his appointment. His aggressive plans for bank retrenchment and bad debt write-off were shot down by both the politicians and banks. Takenaka's uphill battle against a reactionary bureaucracy is hardly surprising, as he inherits senior FSA bureaucrats who were appointed by Yanagisawa. He is also disliked among the bureaucracy for being a better economist and advisor who is closer to the Prime Minister than most other politicians. Takenaka's appointment to head the FSA thus does not necessarily clear the way for tough reforms with any more certainty.

These episodes mark big disappointments in Koizumi's reform drive. It was barely a year before all this happened that a dashing Koizumi came to power on a wave of popularity, promising "structural reform without sanctuary". But it is obvious that Koizumi was fighting a losing battle within a reactionary bureaucratic system.

There is likely to be more reform inertia going forward, curbing the revival of Japan's economic power. Given the strong force of resistance, Japan is not likely to pursue serious banking reform that will lead to closures and layoffs. Instead, she will continue to cheat by forging bank mergers and asking healthy big banks to buy small bad ones. There is a new motivation for doing this, and that is to prevent foreigners from buying major stakes in local banks.

In 2000, the foreign consortium Ripple Wood won the bid for the bankrupt Long-term Credit Bank of Japan (renaming it Shinsei Bank) and turned it into a profitable bank within two years. Foreign investors also took minority stakes in Nippon Credit Bank, now known as Aozora. Despite the success of foreign participation in Japan's bank restructuring process, the FSA seems unhappy with the foreign ownership of Japanese financial institutions. Thus, when the Softbank, an Internet investment group, wanted to sell its 49% holding in 2002 to foreigners including US investment fund Cerberas, the FSA showed reluctance to let Aozora go and introduced tricky criteria to block the deal.

The FSA's intention to keep local institutions within Japanese hands may be patriotism. Indeed, such patriotic reaction (or excuse?) is also shared by many other regional economies when it comes to privatisation. But its inaction to reform may also be just a habit of aversion to change. After all, the banking system involves so many vested interests, including politicians, farmers, property developers, small businesses, and small credit cooperatives. Quite naturally, they want to preserve the old system that gives them credit for funding investment whose risk has been socialised. These vested interests are also crucial supporters of the LDP. The government has no incentive to rock the boat by reforming the system that could hurt their political support.

The lack of resolve to reform has a by-product of impairing the officials' ability to carry out reform properly, even if some leaders want to do something right. There is no better example than Japan's bad loan agency to illustrate the official impotence to tackle structural problems. There were high hopes for the Resolution and Collection Corporation (RCC), the official loan collection agency created in 1999, to help change Japan's awful banks, which carry 150 trillion yen (US$1.2 trillion) of bad loans (as of mid-2002) on their books. But the hope was dissipated completely shortly after the inception of the agency.

The RCC is modelled on America's Resolution Trust Corporation (RTC), which cleaned up after the US savings and loan mess in the late 1980s. But Japan's RCC is no version of the US RTC! The US agency had a limited life; it wound up after the savings and loan crisis was resolved within five years. It was given sufficient power and resources so that it worked efficiently to bring the financial mess under control, at a cost to the American taxpayer that was less than expected. But Japan's RCC has far fewer resources and less authority in tackling a bad-loan problem that dwarfs any in history.

Tokyo may have chosen the right model to deal with its banking problems. But it has run the RCC the wrong way. First, the RCC, funded by government-backed bonds issued by its parent, the Deposit Insurance Corporation, does not have a limited lifespan. Thus, it is not under pressure to act quickly. Although the government set a deadline for it to buy up bad loans from banks by March 2004, it has no deadline for winding up the RCC. This means that disposal of bad debts would drag on, at an unknown cost to Japan's taxpayers.

Second, insufficient resources and incentive problems have hampered the function of the RCC. It has only 2,400 employees, compared with 8,000 that the RTC had. Most of the RCC staff come from the busted financial institutions that created the bulk of the bad loans in the first place. The rest are mostly former bureaucrats. With the economy stuck in the doldrums for over a decade and unemployment rising among white-collar workers, they have no incentive to work fast and then lose their jobs.

Third, bad asset quality makes asset disposal problematic. The RCC has few good assets with which to dilute the bad ones. It took over some five trillion yen of bad loans from bankrupted banks, finance companies, and mortgage corporations, and has recovered about half of these asset values. Yet unlike the US RTC, which took over all good and bad assets of bust savings and loan institutions, the RCC got only the bad assets that the new owners of bust financial institutions did not want. That makes it hard to group assets, by industry or location, into attractive packages for selling in bulk to recoup the losses. In other words, the RCC only functions as a warehouse into which bad assets of all kinds are dumped. So, instead of solving the bad debt problem, the RCC only transfers risk and financial burden from banks to taxpayers, as this bad-debt warehouse is funded by government borrowing!

More fundamentally, it is questionable if the RCC is needed in the first place. This is because the banks have always been free to take rival bids for their loans from private investors. And there is no shortage of private institutions keen to buy bad loans from banks, if the price is right. Since 1999, when they were allowed to apply for licences, more than 60 firms, including foreign investment banks such as Morgan Stanley and Goldman Sachs, have competed with the RCC to buy bad loans from banks. The RCC's role as a bad debt warehouse may be needed to kick-start financial reform, but it should not attempt to restructure companies itself, as it is doing. This is because it does not have the necessary resources and expertise to do the job, which could take years to complete even if it were given the right resources. But some politicians still insist on the RCC taking on the restructuring role without giving it the needed resources. This only reveals Japan's lack of ability, understanding, and vision to make structural changes even if the idea may be the right one.

The sad corollary from all this is that no matter how the RCC might be reformed, it will not be able to help solve Japan's bad loan problem until the banks are forced to act. However, the banks will not act because they fear that selling or writing down more bad debts would leave them badly under-capitalised or even bankrupt. That is why Japan's financial mess has been stuck in dead water for so long. The suggestion that Tokyo should sweeten bad asset sales by buying loans from banks at a premium is nonsense. This is because without fundamental restructuring, that would amount to injection of more public funds to sustain the bad banks.

In a nutshell, years of reform denials have not only raised the cost of inaction but have also made trade offs tougher than they already are. They have also impaired Japan's ability and vision to carry out reform, intensifying the problem of reform inertia. It seems that at every turning point where hard constraints might force reform, the government will continue to manipulate the system to dodge the crunch. The most notable manipulation is the annual propping up of the stock market to boost the banks' capital ratios on their year-end balance sheets. Japanese accounting allows banks to count their stock market investment as capital. Thus, the government buys stocks and pushes up their prices before every fiscal year-end to prevent bank capital ratios from falling below the 8% BIS threshold. This is all done in the name of keeping systemic stability, which has become a handy excuse for putting off painful banking reforms.

For over a decade, Japan has failed or refused to adopt the needed measures to restore economic dynamism. Instead, she has built up enormous debt, her business model is obsolete, her institutions are inefficient, corrupt and riddled with factionalism, and her population is aging rapidly. Reform will only come when the Japanese people demand it or the system collapses. In other words, unless Japan can work magic to make tough choices and implement reforms decisively, it is hard not to write off her economic power in the new economic paradigm. As for Asia, Japan's chronic economic weakness will only intensify deflationary pressures in the region, making its economic transformation more painful on the back of excess capacity and inherent structural woes.

China's Rising Influence

Japan's misfortune is sharply contrasted by China's rise as the darling for foreign investment since the Asian crisis. Significant

FDI inflow to China mirrors rising investor confidence in the Mainland's better reform-growth policy mix. This better policy mix is underscored by creative destruction of the inefficient state sector and improving productivity in the corporate sector (see Chapter 4). The Asian crisis has turned out to be a blessing in disguise for China. By refraining from competitive devaluation, China has regained a lot of political capital that it lost during the June 1989 Tiananmen incident. The expensive RMB relative to other devalued Asian currencies during the Asian crisis had facilitated structural changes by forcing many Chinese manufacturers to raise productivity to offset the currency disadvantage. By learning from the mistakes of other Asian economies without bearing much of the cost, China has also recognised an appropriate sequencing of reform and the importance of maintaining domestic financial stability.

China's gradual stance on financial liberalisation has been a major factor for insulating her from the contagion of the Asian crisis. Beijing's cautious reform attitude has also allowed China to gain economic credibility in the global economy. The Middle Kingdom's economic stability relative to the economic turmoil of her Asian neighbours suggests that it was inappropriate for a developing country to liberalise its capital account transactions too fast. In particular, it was a mistake to have a full open capital account before a country has developed adequate regulatory, institutional, and monetary frameworks to control risk in the domestic financial system. With the benefit of hindsight, Beijing has pursued a correct sequencing of reform by opening China's current account first (in December 1996) before considering opening the capital account. This cautious move has combined with the rapid rising economic might to boost foreign confidence in China's long-term investment outlook, making the Mainland the magnet of foreign investment inflow.

China's relative success in growth and reform will provide a subtle push to Asia's structural reform, thus shaping the region's economic transformation process in the years to come. The Chinese success could create a sense of "Chinese fear" among Asian economies that they would risk being left behind if they do not catch up with China's effort. This will, in turn, create a threat to push Asia onto a structural reform path in order to survive in the new economic paradigm under the Chinese shadow. This sense of fear could even help Japan break her structural reform log jam and unleash a powerful force of economic efficiency as part of the Asian post-bubble economic transformation.

Without structural changes, it will be impossible for Japan to revive herself. The rise of China as Asia's production powerhouse will put huge pressure on Japan's export pricing power and market share. The loss of export power will, in turn, pressure Japan's living standard. Japan has built her wealth through exports. This wealth is no longer growing when market share and pricing power are both shrinking. To slow the decline of this wealth, Japan needs to cut her living costs. This is why cheap Chinese imports have remained popular in Japan's stagnant economy. Japan's imports from China have risen 12 times as fast as her economic growth in the 1990s. Inexpensive Chinese goods, from shitake mushrooms to umbrellas to clothing, will slow down the deterioration of Japan's living standards for many years. But surging Chinese imports have alarmed the Japanese authorities that Japan's economic sovereignty is being threatened.

The Japanese and Asia's perception of a China threat is much like the US perception of a Japanese threat in the 1980s. Then, US companies feared they had fallen behind Japan, whose competitiveness was supposedly assured by superior management techniques, financing, and technology. Now, Japan's fear of being overtaken by China is keenly felt because of the imbedded structural faults in the Japanese system.

China's rising influence in Asia's economic retrenchment process is especially relevant to Japan because there is not much chance of internal forces sparking real reform pressures. Japan's vested interests will continue to resist change. Tokyo is rich enough to continue to bailout the banking system should financial shocks emerge to threaten systemic stability. Nor will there be any push from the jobless demanding change because Tokyo's artificial bailout packages have kept the unemployment rate low at around 3% for years. And Japan has no foreign debt, which shields her from foreign creditors' discipline for change. This thick cloud of reform inertia leaves only a sense of an external shock, a China threat in our context, to give any impetus for Japanese reform.

This situation would be the same as the US in the 1980s, when a sense of a Japan threat prompted the US public and private sectors to study new ways of raising productivity. The resultant changes had helped deliver the longest economic expansion in the US history. It is Japan's turn to take heed of an external (China) threat and turn it into reform momentum. If Japan does not move forward, the China threat that is only a potential danger will become real. Japanese industry will eventually not only relocate assembly operations to China, but also other higher value-added activities, such as design, logistics and management. In the early 1980s, the US was threatened by the Japanese whose average hourly labour cost was only half that of hers. Today, Japan's situation is even worse, as average hourly Japanese labour cost is about 50 times higher than that in China. In the rest of Asia, China still commands the lowest labour cost, except Indonesia. The Chinese pressure is just all too real for Japan and the rest of Asia to ignore.

In terms of demand and supply balance of the regional economy, China has become the manufacturing and processing centre as well as a key end-user market for Asia. China now absorbs as many exports from the rest of Asia as Japan. Evidence suggests that China has become the key force driving Asia's exports. China's purchase of Asian exports has sped up steadily since 2000. The Mainland has surpassed Japan as the largest export market for Asian manufacturers in the region in 2002, accounting for 14% of Asia's total exports compared to an 11% share for Japan.

There are strong reasons to see rising Asian exports to China develop as a trend in the years ahead. WTO requirements will cut Chinese tariffs further, making imports more competitive. Continued economic liberalisation in China will not only raise income, it will also raise Chinese consumer spending power, boosting demand for imports. Meanwhile, Chinese banks are diversifying lending to consumer loans and mortgage lending, giving the Chinese the benefit of financing today's spending with future income for the first time in their lives. Industrial upgrading and rising investment growth will also boost demand for imports of raw materials and capital goods.

Last but not least, the rising importance of intra-regional

trade and the penetration of Chinese goods in the world market will help boost Asian exports to the Middle Kingdom. This is because of China's status as Asia's manufacturing and processing centre. An Acer computer, a Panasonic DVD player, or a pair of Nike running shoes is often made in China. But the Chinese manufacturers have to import raw materials, parts, and other intermediate goods from the rest of Asia for production. Thus, a rise in demand for Chinese and other Asian goods will trigger a chain reaction in Asia's intra-regional trade, which often involves a rise in Asia's exports to China for manufacturing and processing before exporting to the final destination.

Rising penetration of Chinese exports in the global market also has the same chain effect on Asia's exports to China. Typically, China imports parts and other intermediate goods from the rest of Asia, processes them, and then ships the end-products to the rest of the world. A case in point is Taiwan. Her exports to the US have slumped since 1999, but exports to China and Hong Kong have exploded. The reason behind this development is the relocation of major parts of Taiwan's manufacturing business to China. For example, more than 40% of the island's electronics business has already been relocated to the Mainland.

What all this shows is that rising Asian exports to China and China's sharp penetration in the world markets are developing into a trend. They also confirm that Asia's economic integration with the Middle Kingdom since 1990 is accelerating. Manufacturers in the rest of Asia are facing intensifying competition from China. To keep their profit margins from shrinking, high-cost producers have moved to China for low-cost production bases. This also means that the hollowing-out process will be a dominant feature in the new economic paradigm, especially in those more developed Asian economies like Hong Kong, Taiwan, Korea, Singapore, and Japan, where high production cost is a major concern.

Since China has also become an important end-user market for the rest of Asia, her cyclical dynamics will have an increasing impact on the region. A softening Chinese economy is a crucial drag on Asia's growth, while a firming economy is a boost. Finally, the sharp rise in China's market share in global trade is ultimately deflationary for the global economy due to severe

Chinese competitive stress. China's production and marketing pressures will be a key force curbing corporate pricing power in both regional and global manufacturing business. Thus, prolonged disinflation, with periodic deflation, will also be key features in the new paradigm, thanks to the rising influence of China.

The Yen Loses Its Shine in Asia

The advent of the new economic paradigm means that structural forces would be paramount in determining the influence of a national currency in the global and regional systems. Market players' focus on structural factors is a recognition that the value of a currency is often determined by how many opportunities investors see in that economy. If they like the outlook, they buy that currency and put it to use, thus raising its international influence. If they do not like it, the currency will be left in the dumps, experiencing prolonged weakness. With Japanese economic glory declining and Chinese influence rising, it is obvious that long-term structural forces are going against the yen and favouring the RMB.

It is thus only natural to see that the RMB would become more crucial than the yen in affecting Asia's economic well-being in the new paradigm. Deep structural woes, ineffective economic policies, an unsustainable public debt, and denial to reform are negative forces that will keep the Japanese yen in a secular downtrend for many years. So, investors and market players will have more concerns about the impact of a weak yen on the regional markets than a strong one. Nevertheless, due to the sharp decline in Japan's economic influence since the 1990s, the perception that a weakening yen could crash Asia needs to be reassessed.

The conventional thinking is that a weakening yen exacerbates competitive pressure in Asia. Japan's underlying structural woes, huge public debt overhang, and zero interest rates have boxed the Japanese authorities into a policy corner with few options other than to let the yen fall to prevent an economic collapse. Meanwhile, the fall in Asia's reliance on Japan as the major export destination and the rise in Japan's reliance on exports to Asia since the 1990s have transformed Asia from a dependent of the Japanese economy to a competitor of it. Asia now competes with Japan in many key industries, such as auto, electronics, machinery, semiconductors, and shipping. The region as a whole also accounts for a much larger share of US imports than Japan. This suggests that Asia was out-competing many Japanese products in the third markets, notably the US. As evident from the US trade data, non-Japan Asian imports accounted for 20% of total US imports in 1992. This share rose to 23% in 2000. On the other hand, the share of Japanese goods fell 6% from 18% of total US imports to 12% during the same period.

The fear of a falling yen crashing Asia thus goes like this. As a competitor of Japan, Asian authorities would react to the competitive threat of a falling yen, thus risking competitive currency devaluation pushing Asia into recession. When China is dragged into this, she would be forced to devalue the RMB in response to the region's "beggar thy neighbour" policy, where one country's devaluation triggers a similar policy elsewhere. This outcome would be quite destabilising, as the RMB has been seen as an anchor of stability in Asia since the 1997/1998 regional crisis.

Given Asia's structural problems, the threat of a yen-induced currency crisis could be serious. As discussed in Chapter 2, Asia's cheating on reform means that the old economic excesses have not been completely purged so that many of the structural woes still remain. These structural problems have blunted the effects of monetary policy in many Asian countries due to their dysfunctional financial systems that distort the monetary transmission mechanism. Ineffective monetary policy has in turn placed extra reliance on government spending to boost economic growth.

However, fiscal policy has also become inflexible, as Asian governments have been running up large fiscal deficits since the Asian crisis. Both Northeast and Southeast Asian economies have seen fiscal deficits stuck at or above 3% of their GDP. According to the international norm, a fiscal deficit above 3% of GDP is deemed unsustainable and will lead to major economic troubles, such as crowding out of private investment, surging inflation, and worsening current account balance. A swift improvement in the region's fiscal books is unlikely, given the prolonged deflationary environment in the economic transformation period. In other words, Asian governments are hitting a fiscal wall, which is impairing their ability to boost growth. Thus, exchange rate depreciation, with the hope of boosting exports, becomes an alternative policy tool to prevent economic decline. This underscores the fears of competitive devaluation stemming from a weak yen.

Nonetheless, the fear that a weakening yen will crash Asia is exaggerated. The sharp decline in Japan's economic impact on Asia suggests that the magnitude of any Japanese domino effect on Asia had dropped sharply. Further, most of Asia (sans Japan) is now better equipped to weather external or foreign exchange shocks than it was before the 1997/1998 regional crisis. The region has accumulated more foreign exchange reserves (40% higher in 2002 than pre-crisis levels) and currencies are cheaper than the Japanese yen on a trade-weighted basis after adjustments for relative inflation rates. Foreign (including yen-denominated) debt levels are much lower, making Asia less susceptible to withdrawal by foreign creditors.

Since the Asian crisis, most regional economies, except China, Hong Kong, Malaysia, and to a large extent Taiwan, have adopted the floating exchange rate regime. This flexible regime has given the regional monetary authorities the flexibility to boost economic growth by cutting interest rates even at times of currency volatility. Such flexibility did not exist during the pre-crisis fixed exchange rate regime because the authorities had no control of interest rates. Monetary policy was purely a function of exchange rate pressures. The authorities had to raise interest rates, thus curbing capital outflow, to keep the exchange rate fixed when the currency was under selling pressure. On the other hand, they had to cut rates to stem appreciation pressure when the currency was under buying pressure. Thus, the fixed exchange rate regime deprived the authorities of any monetary policy flexibility.

Short-term depreciation pressure on Asian currencies during the region's economic transformation period may not necessarily hurt the underlying economies and markets if depreciation remains orderly. Exchange rate flexibility could help reduce volatility in the real economy. This is because in a deflationary environment, currency depreciation will help raise nominal GDP growth by boosting exports. It will also help raise profits when overseas earnings and foreign trade proceeds are translated back into the local weaker currency. A rise in nominal GDP will in turn help alleviate the profit squeeze brought about by the erosion of pricing power in the new paradigm.

A weakening yen is also unlikely to push China to devalue. China remains a closed economy, with a small external sector and a closed capital account. These will only change slowly, despite China's WTO accession. Thus, the impact of the RMB exchange rate on domestic economic growth will remain relatively small in the medium term, reducing the temptation by Chinese authorities to use currency devaluation as a growth tool. Further, Chinese exports are competitive, as seen in their strong gains in the US export market share since the Asian crisis even without currency devaluation. China's huge US$260 billion strong foreign exchange reserves (as of mid-2002) and strict capital controls will continue to serve as stabilising factors for her exchange rate regime in the medium term.

All this is not to say that a sick Japanese economy and a weakening yen would not have any impact. In general, countries with relatively low economic ties with Japan will be less affected by the direct impact of an ailing Japanese economy. These economic ties can be approximated by the amount of exports to Japan and the amount of FDI received from Japan. Figure 5.2 plots the combined export and FDI exposure to Japan of Asian economies. The percentage of exports to Japan is shown on the horizontal axis and the percentage of FDI received from Japan on the vertical axis. The further away this combination from the point of origin, zero, the larger the Asian economy's exposure to Japan. This evidence shows that Malaysia, Korea, the Philippines, and China have relatively small exposure to Japan, and thus seem relatively immune to an ailing Japan economy compared with Hong Kong, Singapore, and Taiwan.

Nevertheless, the overall impact of a weakening yen will still be painful for Asia because it could intensify the decline in tradable goods prices, weaken global pricing power, and squeeze

Figure 5.2 Asia's Economic Exposure to Japan

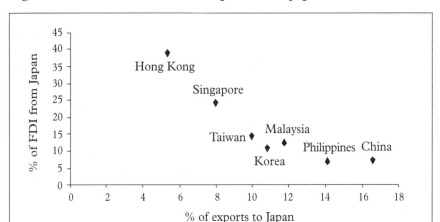

manufacturers' margins. Prolonged decline in the yen could also blunt Asian authorities' monetary stimulus to boost economic growth, as the yen-induced deflationary shock destroys wealth, confidence, and hence demand growth in the region. Despite China's overall limited exposure to Japan, a falling yen could still be painful for the Chinese exporters when Beijing keeps operating a *de facto* RMB peg against the US dollar and refuses to devalue.

If the Chinese keep their no-devaluation pledge as decline in the yen drags down other Asian currencies, something will have to give to keep Chinese exports competitive. And that will likely be Chinese profits because the falling yen will also push down tradable goods prices across Asia, forcing Chinese exporters to slash prices to remain competitive. This will, in turn, squeeze Chinese profit margins. The very response of Chinese exporters slashing prices will only reinforce China as a source of deflation in Asia. In other words, Asian manufacturers will not enjoy a revival of pricing power under the combination of a weakening yen and a fixed RMB exchange rate. Rather, such a combination would risk deepening deflation, making the regional backdrop tougher for Asia's economic transition in the new economic paradigm.

In terms of currencies, those that have a high correlation with movement of the yen will face the biggest downward pressure if the yen falls. If experience is any guide, these include the New Taiwan dollar and the Korean Won (see Table 5.1). They have a high tendency to move in the same direction with the yen in at least seven times out of ten. This is not surprising since Taiwan and South Korea are Japan's main export rivals.

Despite the decline in Japan's influence in Asia, the RMB will not replace the yen in the short term because Japan remains by far the largest net creditor in the world. She also makes up over two-thirds of the region's economy in Asia. China will only replace Japan as an economic powerhouse over the longer term. But this may not be too far away, given the accelerating economic integration between Asia and China, and given China's rapid rise as a major trading power under the WTO. It will not be surprising if China overtakes Japan as the major regional economic engine before Japan could dig herself out of structural woes.

Table 5.1 Correlation with the Japanese Yen (1999–2001)

Currency	Correlation
Philippine peso	−0.07
Hong Kong dollar	0
Chinese renminbi	0
Malaysian ringgit	0
Thai baht	0.05
Indonesian rupiah	0.42
Singapore dollar	0.47
Korean won	0.73
New Taiwan dollar	0.78

There are solid reasons why we can expect China's economic power to continue to grow. Much of her growth so far has been very basic catch-up. The reforms undertaken, starting in 1978, have unleashed market and entrepreneurial forces that were suppressed during the Mao years. These forces had also suffered in the decades preceding economic liberation due to the poor governance of the Kuomintang and the state of civil war. China's resolve to grow will only get stronger in the new economic era. Her number one priority is to create jobs as the 750-million labour force is hugely under-utilised. Over half of this labour force was educated after the Cultural Revolution in the 1960s. They are well-informed of the high living standards in other countries and demand similar opportunities. China turns out 2.5 million college graduates every year and she welcomes foreign investment as the main source of industrial upgrading and efficiency improvement.

China's positive outlook only highlights Japan's grim prospects, a large part of which is of Japan's own making. Japan's behaviour since the late 1980s has contrasted sharply with her open attitude in the mid-19th century. In the 1860s, Japan chose to open up and became quite a remarkable society in almost every aspect. But in the 1990s, she had lost this positive and open attitude. She has stifled creativity and her entrepreneurial spirit by refusing to change. As a result, she has stagnated in a spirit of introverted decadence. Since Japan has yet to formulate her revival strategy, she is likely to remain a marginal player both in the regional and global arenas.

On the other hand, China's influence on shaping Asia's economic transformation, in terms of production pattern, pricing power, and structural reforms, will increasingly be felt by regional economies in the new economic paradigm at the expense of Japan. Chinese foreign exchange policy will also carry an increasing weight in influencing international currency policies and movements. Indeed, the powerful Group of Seven's (G7) finance authorities have been increasing their consultation with the Chinese authorities on various global monetary and financial affairs since the Asian crisis. The best scenario would be one in which China and Japan embrace economic reforms and free trade so that both economies would be anchored in regional development. This would also allow Japan to keep her influence for a longer period of time. However, as long as Tokyo is stuck in a socio-economic-political vacuum, China's influence will dominate Asia's economic development in the new economic era.

Chapter 6

Case Study 1 – China's Pressure on Hong Kong

As case studies for China's influence on Asia's transformation in the new economic paradigm, we shall examine Chinese pressure on Hong Kong in this chapter and Taiwan in the next. Being part of the Greater China economy with close business and investment ties with the Mainland, China's rising economic fortune should in principle benefit Hong Kong and Taiwan directly. However, these "tigers" have suffered significant economic decline as China flexes her economic muscle. For example, both were in economic recession in 2001, while China celebrated her entry into the World Trade Organisation (WTO) and her robust 7.3% annual economic growth rate.

Both Hong Kong and Taiwan are seen as having strong economic fundamentals that should help them weather external shocks. Nevertheless, they have suffered miserable economic malaise since 2001, just when the world was looking at how China's economic strength would benefit the whole Greater China economy. The Hong Kong government has blindly taken a naive official line of "China well, Hong Kong well" without even pondering the nature and root causes of Hong Kong's problems. While Hong Kong may benefit from China's success in the long term, it will not be smooth-sailing in the short term. Indeed, Hong Kong's and Taiwan's experience serves to highlight the structural stress that China's rising economic power could inflict in Asia. Their unpleasant experience suggests further that even the strong "tiger" economies could lose their stripes under the Chinese shadow. They must reinvent themselves to survive in the new paradigm. If not, what is potentially short-term decline could turn into long-term economic decadence, just like Japan.

Double Whammy

The problems in Hong Kong are especially puzzling. Five years after the Asian crisis, the Hong Kong banking system was still flooded with ample liquidity. The public's affordability to buy houses had risen to high levels not seen in 14 years. Hong Kongers had been sitting on a big pile of cash since the regional debacle, with total bank deposits amounting to HK$3.42 trillion (or over 260% of GDP). Interest rates had fallen to historic lows of less than 2% in the inter-bank market, underscoring the rise in housing affordability and cheap investment cost. Narrow money supply had been rising at double-digit rates, suggesting that people had been shifting money into their demand deposits and holding an increasing amount of notes and coins. This sharp rise in the public's holding of liquid assets should be a sign for spending to take off. And all this should provide a positive wealth effect for boosting consumer demand.

Yet, the territory's economy and stock market only rebounded briefly since the 1997/1998 regional crisis. The economy had slipped back into recession by late 2001 for the second time in three years. A prolonged deflationary trap of falling goods and asset prices, shrinking consumption and soaring unemployment followed. In nominal terms, Hong Kong's economy contracted between 1999 and 2002. Intensifying deflation, with consumer prices falling at an average 3.5% p.a. and a distorted credit mechanism plagued the economy. The wealth destruction process of deflation killed public confidence, trapping private demand and investment in dead water, despite the territory's proud claim of having the healthiest banking system in Asia, with the exception of Singapore. In 2002, unemployment had soared to a historic high of 8% of the labour force, an unbearable experience for a city which had never seen an unemployment rate of more than 1% before. Plunging interest rates had failed to halt the contraction of nominal GDP and bank loans, with the latter averaging −13.5% a year since the Asian crisis. Rising property prices were a key ingredient of the city's growth, but property values had never recovered from a 65% drop in 1998.

All this points to a "liquidity trap" in Hong Kong, a condition where ample liquidity and record low interest rates have failed to revive economic growth. Such miserable economic experience has created a growing sense of helplessness in the territory. This is reflected most dramatically by a jump of more than 30% in suicides by working-age people in 2001. Cases of self-induced suffocation, done by burning coal briquettes in sealed rooms, had increased at such an alarming rate between 2001 and 2002 that charcoal bags sold in supermarkets were emblazoned with suicide-prevention hotline numbers. There seems to be a complete loss of faith in Hong Kong's economic future by the public and the government (despite the official denial). Reflecting this loss of confidence is the Hong Kong government's initiatives to seek Beijing's help to salvage the city's economy, such as preferential treatment for Hong Kong companies and government-sponsored trade delegations.

The government's argument for going to Beijing is to provide a "helping hand" to open doors to the Mainland – a place where politicians and businessmen are often one and the same. But the government's new roles as lobbyist and relationship broker are inspiring some entrepreneurs to curry favour, risking the creation of a so-called "Santa Claus economy" that relies on handouts from its patron to the north. Examples are easy to find. They include Hong Kong banks seeking regulatory waivers on the Mainland and a proposal by the city's main accounting association that Beijing extends trade advantages only to Hong Kong companies run by ethnic Chinese.

What's wrong with this city, which was once admired by the world as the best example of *laissez-faire* economics? It is easy to point to high costs, failed education, and price pressure from China, as the city's economy becomes increasingly integrated with the Mainland's. Yet these explanations seem inadequate. Looking deeper into Hong Kong's economy, the problem lies in a double whammy of cyclical economic downturn and structural transformation. The cyclical pains are obvious. The Asian crisis of 1997/1998 has unleashed significant deflationary pressures throughout Asia, as slumping demand aggravates the problem of excess capacity. The synchronised global economic slowdown in 2001 and 2002 had only aggravated Hong Kong's cyclical pains, as foreign trade, which is Hong Kong's economic lifeline, contracted. With the external sector accounting for two-and-a-half times the size of GDP, the negative domino impact of a decline in foreign trade on Hong Kong's economy is huge. Thus, despite four years of falling prices that are supposed to increase real purchasing power, Hong Kong's consumer spending has not been able to sustain a recovery after contracting by an average of 15% a year during the Asian crisis.

Despite the territory's well-earned prestige as a net foreign creditor, its domestic debt burden is heavy, with a loan-to-GDP ratio of 200%! And this poses a problem because deflation has significantly raised Hong Kong's real domestic debt burden. Prolonged deflation has also created falling price expectations, prompting households to postpone spending. Meanwhile, falling prices are supposed to raise real wages, as nominal wages have remained sticky in the face of deflation. Higher real wages, in turn, are supposed to raise purchasing power and, hence, consumer spending. However, the deflationary process in Hong Kong has backfired. The sharp rise in real wages, which grew from an annual rate of 1% in 1998 to 7% in 2000, on the back of chronic erosion of pricing power, has prompted companies to cut costs and layoff workers in order to protect margins. This has weakened job confidence and spending ability, eroded pricing power further, and forced companies to cut jobs again, thus pushing the economy into a deflationary spiral.

Structural Woes

The structural pains are subtler, and they have a lot to do with China. Integrating high-cost Hong Kong economy with low-cost Mainland is creating structural deflation for Hong Kong, as the pressure of price equalisation between the two economies intensifies. Hong Kong's back-office jobs, from telephone operators to accountants, have begun moving to the southern province of Guangdong, much the way manufacturing jobs emigrated in the 1980s. Its consumers have followed suit, clogging border checkpoints trying to get to Guangdong's cheaper malls, cinemas, restaurants, and karaoke bars. All this has fuelled deflation and unemployment in the territory. At a per capita income of US$24,000 a year versus China's US$900, Hong Kong has to expand further into high value-added services to sustain income growth under China's competitive pressure. Further, China's entry into the WTO has lessened the importance of Hong Kong as a window to the Middle Kingdom. The challenge for Hong Kong is one of reinvention, but the city's government has failed to put together a credible plan.

While Hong Kong prides itself on being adaptive to changing times with high entrepreneurial spirits, the trouble this time around is totally different. The economic transformation ahead needs skills that are quite different from the trade and manufacturing activities that Hong Kong is used to. So, there is an urgency to change these conventional entrepreneurial skills. But old habits die hard and thinking outside the box is no easy task for an economy that is known for taking orders from its master but not for problem-solving. Aggravating Hong Kong's confusion is its education system that is deficient of creativity and communications and problem-solving skills. Thus, the combination of the urgency to change and a poor economic backdrop has created a strong sense of insecurity and helplessness, which contributes to the liquidity trap conditions that have submerged the economy in a prolonged quagmire.

Separately, China's economic liberalisation and her elevation to the global financial stage have exposed structural problems in Hong Kong's corporate sector. As investors in China can attest, corporate governance is non-existent on the Mainland. On the other hand, Hong Kong seems to have enjoyed high international trust in this regard, and it aims at holding itself out as an example for the rest of Asia. This is why many investors still see tremendous value in Hong Kong's financial markets as the preferred place to list Chinese companies and to buy Chinese stocks. But they should look again. Thanks to China's growing importance in the global investment arena, the scrutiny on Hong Kong's corporate and financial framework has intensified. And the findings are not pleasant because Hong Kong is far from meeting the perception of being a model of corporate governance.

Hong Kong is ranked among the best in surveys of Asian corporate governance. For example, in a study in January 2002, international credit-rating agency Standard and Poors ranked Hong Kong's corporate governance only after Singapore in Asia. However, such a high ranking is only relative to other generally opaque Asian economies. Hong Kong actually has few companies that practise the perceived world-class corporate governance. One need only look to examples such as the Peregrine Investment and Guangdong Holdings scandals to find Hong Kong's "junior Enrons". Compared with the US and the UK, Hong Kong companies are reluctant to disclose financial details, especially executive remuneration. Listed firms in Singapore are required to report quarterly. Even in China, a similar requirement came into force at the start of 2002. But Hong Kong regulations only require semi-annual reporting. Further, most of the city's companies are family-owned, which hampers the rights of the minority shareholders.

The key problem of corporate governance in Hong Kong is the lack of truly independent non-executive directors. Family members or management themselves often dominate company boards. This makes it difficult for truly independent scrutiny of managers' performance and operations transparency. Those companies that have independent directors often picked them from the group of professionals who are known to the management executives, such as their friends, lawyers, accountants, or bankers. Nepotism is prevalent.

The advantage of such a system is that the directors all know and trust each other. But it is also like cronyism such that an independent director will not have the incentive to raise any issues that the executives or controlling shareholders do not want to hear. To meet international investors' expectations of having a clean and effective corporate system, Hong Kong is under imminent pressure to change its corporate structure. However, the lack of leadership and resolve to do so on the back of rising interest to directly invest in China has only added to anxiety and confusion among Hong Kong's communities. The territory is risking being bypassed by foreign investors.

What Kills Confidence?

Contrary to conventional wisdom in the local business community, Hong Kong's confidence crisis is not a result of the "negative net worth" effect or the Hong Kong dollar peg. Meanwhile, the Hong Kong government has had to shoulder most of the responsibility for aggravating the loss of confidence in the territory. Let us look at the negative net worth issue first. It is true that deflation has badly hurt property owners who were locked in double-digit mortgage rates during the bubble years in the late 1980s and early 1990s. With post-bubble property values falling by an average of 60% below their purchase prices during the peak in 1998, the market crash has created a class of "negative equity" property owners.

Wealth destruction, huge mortgage debt burden, and income insecurity have crashed the confidence and spending power of this group of asset owners. Adding fuel to fire, some local media have exploited the collapse in property prices to "create" news headlines, stirring more fears among the public. But these irresponsible reports have grossly exaggerated the issue of negative net worth because this group of asset owners accounts for no more than 80,000 or about 1% of Hong Kong's seven million population. The group is hardly a critical mass that can crash the economy.

The crisis is not the fault of the Hong Kong dollar peg either, despite the common thinking among local businesses that the currency peg had killed Hong Kong's competitiveness by making its goods and services dearer than its regional rivals. The choice of an exchange rate regime for Hong Kong is not the subject of this book. But we can briefly consider the arguments for Hong Kong's currency peg as a background for our understanding of the issues here. There are solid fundamental arguments to support that the currency peg is appropriate for Hong Kong.

A fixed exchange rate better suits a small open economy, like Hong Kong, than a large closed economy, like China, because the trade sector of the former has a much larger share of GDP. Thus, the cost of currency fluctuations under a floating exchange rate could be very high for a small open economy. Notably, high foreign exchange volatility makes business planning for both inward and outward foreign trade and investment difficult, if not impossible. Further, domestic monetary policy in such an economy is powerless to offset any external shocks. The best course of action that the government of a small open economy can undertake is to eliminate foreign exchange risk to facilitate foreign trade and investment by pegging its currency against a credible hard currency. That was what Hong Kong did in 1985, when the local dollar was pegged at a fixed rate of HK$7.8 per US dollar. The aim was to diffuse political uncertainty resulting from the Sino-British talks on the future of Hong Kong.

Given the currency peg, Hong Kong's economic pains are the natural adjustment process of the system. Since Hong Kong's exchange rate cannot fall when others do, local prices (including goods, services, labour, and asset prices) have to fall to keep its competitiveness. Indeed, local deflation has pushed Hong Kong's real effective exchange rate back to where it was during the Asian crisis. This refutes the claims that the Hong Kong dollar was significantly overvalued and hurting Hong Kong exports. The city's real effective exchange rate is the inflation-adjusted, trade-weighted exchange rate against its major trading partners. Basically, lower inflation reduces domestic production costs and leads to a fall in the real effective exchange rate. Thus, the currency peg-induced deflation in local prices has helped offset Hong Kong's loss of competitiveness due to the inability of the local dollar to fall while other Asian currencies depreciate. It is true, though, that the rise in China's economic clout has intensified and prolonged this painful domestic adjustment process under the currency peg.

If the Hong Kong dollar peg were a confidence killer, we would not have seen a steady rise in the number of regional headquarters and foreign affiliates in Hong Kong during the Asian crisis. This favourable trend is depicted in Figure 6.1. Data from the Hong Kong Census and Statistics Department shows that the number of foreign companies setting up regional headquarters in the territory rose from 816 in 1996, the year before the Asian crisis, to 944 in 2001. Meanwhile, the number of foreign firms setting up affiliated shops in Hong Kong also rose from 1,491 to 2,293 during the same period. Further, if

Figure 6.1 Regional HQ's and Foreign Offices in Hong Kong

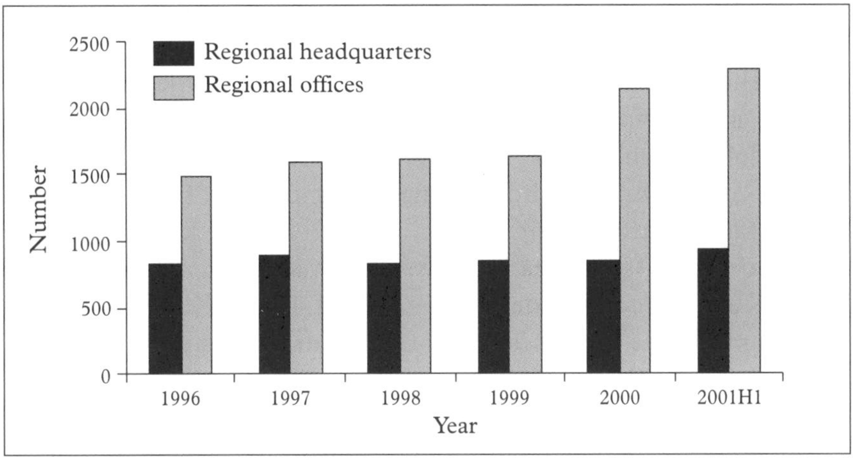

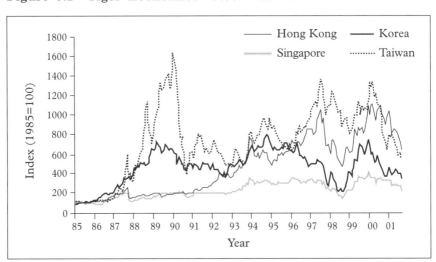

Source: HK Census and Statistics Department

investors did not like the Hong Kong dollar peg, Hong Kong's stock market would not have outperformed the other Asian "tiger" markets, except Taiwan, since the inception of the Hong Kong dollar peg in 1985. The spectacular performance of the Hong Kong stock market is seen clearly in Figure 6.2.

Abandoning the peg would not necessarily benefit Hong Kong. Given the prospects of a prolonged and painful economic

Figure 6.2 Tiger Economies' Stock Market Indices

transformation in the new economic paradigm under China's shadow, unpegging will likely result in a sharp fall in the Hong Kong dollar. Since foreign exchange rate movement has a habit of overshooting the equilibrium value, especially when there is a change in the foreign exchange regime, unpegging the Hong Kong dollar would lead to depreciation overshoot and surging import costs. This will hurt Hong Kong on two fronts. First, a sharp fall in the Hong Kong dollar will risk competitive devaluation in Asia, negating any perceived gains in exports for Hong Kong. Second, due to the size of Hong Kong's imports, which amount to over 100% of GDP, surging import costs will actually hurt Hong Kong's competitiveness, not boost its exports, by increasing production costs.

Floating the Hong Kong dollar is also not a viable option at least for a few more years. This is because Hong Kong lacks a proper central bank to conduct credible monetary policy. The Hong Kong Monetary Authority (HKMA) is not a central bank, but a sentinel of the currency peg and a bank regulator with central bank ambitions. None of the senior management at the HKMA has the appropriate education or experience to conduct sensible monetary policy. The comments of the late Merton Miller, Nobel laureate in economics, at a Legislative Council hearing in Hong Kong in November 1998 revealed the inexperience of the HKMA managers. He noted that Joseph Yam, the head of the HKMA, does not have appropriate educational and professional economics backgrounds. Both had their wires crossed when discussing economic issues in the legislature. Hence, before unpegging the Hong Kong dollar, the HKMA must be reformed and restaffed. But such a step will surely meet severe resistance from vested interests.

Since Hong Kong has a currency link system like Argentina's, many have compared Hong Kong with Argentina, especially during times of economic stress. Many investors have feared, intuitively, that the fate of the two currency boards was linked together. This is inappropriate. The 29% devaluation of the Argentine peso in November 2001 heralded the end of Argentina's currency board system. But the Hong Kong dollar did not experience any significant selling pressure. The comparison is somewhat premature at this time. Argentina was and still is plagued by the deadly combination of high foreign debt, deep deflation, a bankrupt government, and an overvalued currency. But Hong Kong is not. Hong Kong is a net foreign creditor, despite its high domestic debt load, and the Hong Kong government has enjoyed huge fiscal reserves for years. Indeed, when Argentina finally scrapped her peso peg in January 2002, the Hong Kong dollar peg stood like an island in the storm. There was no significant selling pressure detected in the local banking system.

The choice of an exchange rate regime is often a political decision because there are always arguments for and against a particular regime. Hong Kong's currency peg arrangement made good sense during the volatile pre-handover years and straddling, as it did, a remarkable period of growth. There are also good reasons for it to stay in the future as an appropriate monetary instrument to foster growth confidence. In a nutshell, the Hong Kong dollar peg is like a religion – if you believe in it, it is good; if not, it is bad.

The economic debate about the pros and cons of the currency peg system changes according to the fluctuations of the business cycle. This is because at a time when the US and Hong Kong cycles are moving in the same direction, the currency peg benefits Hong Kong by importing the appropriate monetary policy prescription from the US to regulate the local economy. On the other hand, if the US and Hong Kong economies are out of sync, what is a right policy for the US may be a wrong prescription for Hong Kong.

Consider the US economic recession in the early 1990s. The US Federal Reserve's response was to cut interest rates to boost growth. But that policy only worsened Hong Kong's inflation problem at a time when its overheated economy needed interest rate hikes to cool off. Thus, the calls from Hong Kong's business community to scrap the peg because it hurts business are missing the point. Economic grounds often need not form the central basis for the authorities' decision to keep or abandon the currency peg.

Now let us turn to the confidence issue. The loss of public confidence in Hong Kong has a lot to do with system failure, which is reflected by the lack of government credibility. The

Chief Executive, Tung Chee Wah, and those around him do not seem to have high regard for what others have to say about the core issues of Hong Kong such as the civil service, the judiciary, and professionals. He has taken the view of a traditional Chinese businessman – that they are creating Hong Kong, they have the links on the Mainland, and that is all that is needed to govern Hong Kong. Viewing it differently, it seems the government has tried to govern the city with an aristocratic style but it lacks the vision and capability of the aristocrats to make decisions!

The economic malaise of this wealthy city on the back of a thriving hinterland in the immediate north highlights the vulnerability of an economy with weak leadership facing a strengthening China. The government's zigzagging policies, indecision, and the lack of accountability and vision have aggravated Hong Kong's confidence crisis. Five years of official efforts to micro-manage the property market decline since the reversion of Hong Kong to China in 1997 has seen countless policy revisions. The official manipulation has changed the rules of the game and shaken investor confidence. Ask property agents in London, Sydney, Vancouver and New York, and they will tell you Hong Kongers still provide a large share of their clientele. Hong Kong's expatriate, and even local, children are filling up some of the world's dearest private/international schools. The point is that there is no lack of money in Hong Kong, but the money is just not being spent there!

The opening up of China, and the mounting competitive stress that she brings, has questioned Hong Kong's status as an attractive haven for wealth creation and preservation. The question becomes more acute when the public and investors are dealing with a weak leadership suffering from administrative failures. From this context, loss of confidence in Hong Kong runs beyond a cyclical decline in expectations. Under the city's ineffective leadership, the basic terms of market engagement are changed on a near monthly basis. It is thus not surprising that income is funnelled offshore. With China in the picture again, who provides cheaper alternatives with improving quality for consumption and investment, that quickens the emigration of Hong Kong's wealth.

The fight between the local developers and the government

over the Home Ownership Scheme (HOS) is the most visible
evidence of zigzagging policies, indecision, and the lack of vision
of the Hong Kong government. By undercutting the HOS-
subsidised homes for sale programme and offering potential
buyers cash bonuses for backing out of their HOS purchases,
developers are seeking to kill a programme that sits at the heart
of the official policy agenda. The government first introduced the
HOS programme in 1997 after the handover of Hong Kong to
China. It set a target of building 85,000 units of subsidised
housing each year for the public. But it failed to see the negative
supply impact on property prices, which was aggravated by the
Asian crisis. The developers were furious and were pressuring the
government to back off from the programme. The government
tried in vain to stop the decline in property prices by halting
construction once every year since 1998. It finally quietly
scrapped the 85,000 target in 2002.

The system failure has raised the question of who will invest
in the very sectors that the Hong Kong government picks as
winners, including logistics and transport and high-tech centres,
if tomorrow sees some public initiatives launching a rival project
padded with subsidised land? Office landlords already harbour a
grudge against the government, who has lured tenants willing to
pay the market rate for rent take up subsidised government
office projects, such as the Cyberport and Science Park. Further,
China is also developing similar sectors, such as logistics and
high tech, to compete with Hong Kong. The Mainland is also
offering cheaper labour and land to lure investment. Under such
circumstances, it is hardly surprising that Hong Kong's capital is
being deployed elsewhere, local confidence has collapsed, and
the economy is being crushed.

Erosion of a Traditional Role

Hong Kong will lose its traditional role as a trade and
investment conduit between China and the rest of the world over
the longer term as the Mainland continues to open up. That is
why the traditional entrepreneurial skills in manufacturing and
trading that Hong Kong is used to are no longer enough for
survival. But even in the short- to medium-term, the entry of

China and Taiwan into the WTO, which will eventually make
direct trade and transport between them a reality, will accelerate
the demise of Hong Kong's role as a middleman. Those who
think otherwise, including the government, are just kidding
themselves – another example of denial!

Trade between China and Taiwan is routed via Hong Kong
because direct trade, transport, and communications across the
Taiwan Strait have been banned since 1949. In 1987, authorities
on both sides of the Strait decided to allow trading only via a
third region, practically Hong Kong. Annual indirect cross-strait
trade via Hong Kong has grown to over US$10 billion a year
from just US$4 billion in 1990. Direct trade is just a matter of
time after China and Taiwan's entry into the WTO. A complete
loss of this indirect trade business after the direct-trade ban is
lifted will amount to an estimated 5.7% of Hong Kong's annual
total exports, or 6% of GDP, a non-trivial amount that will only
aggravate the territory's restructuring pains.

Signs have emerged for direct China–Taiwan trade. In April
1997, Taiwan opened up Kaoshiung as an offshore trans-
shipment centre, allowing foreign ships to sail directly between
Taiwan and the Mainland. In response, China also opened up
two ports in Xiamen and Fuzhou to link with Kaoshiung. In
2000, Taiwan allowed three more outlying islands to directly
trade with China. The establishment of the Kaoshiung trans-
shipment centre has already shrunk the share of China–Taiwan
trade reexported via Hong Kong to 36% of Hong Kong's total
reexports in 2000 from 63% in 1993.

Hong Kong's middleman role is not limited to the trade
sector. Under the ban on direct transport, there are no direct
flights between Taiwan and the Mainland. Taiwanese are required
to travel via a third point, such as Hong Kong or Macau. The
number of Taiwanese visiting Hong Kong amounts to 2.5 million
a year in recent years. They account for 20% of all tourist
arrivals in Hong Kong. Among these Taiwanese visitors, about
half are registered as transiting from Hong Kong to the
Mainland. If there were direct cross-strait links, these transit
visitors could bypass Hong Kong, representing at least a possible
10% drop in Hong Kong's tourist arrivals.

The WTO membership for China and Taiwan has already

tightened the ties between them and made some banking arrangements easier across the Taiwan Strait. Each government has given financiers the green light to tighten links and streamline services, helping entrepreneurs who have been doing business by largely ignoring politics between Taiwan and China over the past decades. Some of the direct finance dealings will threaten the mainstays of Hong Kong banking, such as the growing practice of writing direct letters of credit (LCs) and direct wire transfers. LCs are a basic trade-finance tool with a bank guaranteeing, for a fee, that a buyer will honour payments to a seller. LCs are a crucial item on Hong Kong's banking menu of trade services.

In the past, China and Taiwan could not have a direct banking relationship. So, they had to go through a third party bank, usually a Hong Kong bank, to facilitate cross-strait trade transactions. But in early 2002, after China and Taiwan were admitted into the WTO, Taiwan banks began sidestepping the Hong Kong banking system and wrote LCs for Chinese trade directly because the practice was made acceptable under the WTO. Not requiring a third party bank in Hong Kong saves time and money. For example, ANZ-Taiwan, the Taipei branch of Australia and New Zealand Banking Group Ltd., charges a fee of about 0.1% of the transaction value on the Taiwan side for arranging an LC for Chinese trade. Its counterpart, the Bank of China in the Mainland, charges 0.125% from the other side. If this were done the old way, the middleman bank that processed it through Hong Kong would have to tack an additional 0.3%. Transaction time is also cut to about a day, from as much as a week.

Financing trade that moves through Hong Kong generates over US$100 billion in business for Hong Kong banks. Further, besides the LC-trade finance business, Chinese and Taiwanese banks have forged closer ties in other ways that reduce Hong Kong's middleman role. For example, after obtaining permission in early 2002 to open representative offices in China, Taiwanese banks have less need to rely on Hong Kong banks to help drum up Chinese business. And a growing direct remittance business, like LC operations, also means lesser fees for Hong Kong banks. The long-term blow to Hong Kong's banking business could be significant. Direct financial links between Taiwan and China thus forces Hong Kong to reinvent itself even in its traditionally strong area of finance. This highlights another aspect of China's pressure on the territory's economic outlook under the new paradigm.

Last but not least, Hong Kong's intermediary role in investment will also be eroded. Taiwanese companies that use Hong Kong as a stepping-stone to China will either have a nominal corporate entity or a physical presence in Hong Kong to fulfill Taipei's requirements of indirect investment in the Mainland. Those who have a physical presence in Hong Kong have in addition used its business and financial facilities to support their operations or serve customers in the Mainland. But this intermediary role for Taiwan's investment will be lost after the establishment of direct links with China.

The economic damages in Hong Kong stemming from the loss of indirect trade, investment, and transport business may still be manageable in the short term. Much of it may be offset by the increase in reexports from China through Hong Kong, as the Mainland's foreign trade volume expands after her WTO accession. This reexport trade business currently amounts to over US$90 billion each year, or 54% of Hong Kong's GDP. Others have found comfort in Hong Kong's effort to develop itself into a regional transport hub to keep its foreign trade value under the shadow of China.

However, this thinking is shortsighted and Hong Kong's efforts to boost the transport and logistics sector, though a step in the right direction, may not be enough to save the day. Over the longer term, the principal threat to the territory's regional centre status comes not from Singapore, Taiwan, or the Philippines, but from China. Take air transport as an example. In the past, the threat to Hong Kong's Chek Lap Kok International Airport, still the largest in the world as of 2002, from southern Chinese airports was dismissed. People used to write off the Mainland airports as serious rivals due to their primitive infrastructure and a laughable approach to ground handling and airport management.

Not anymore because Chinese competition is catching up fast. Guangzhou's new Baiyun International Airport, operational as of 2003, is China's largest and most advanced international airport. By 2010, the airport is expected to process 25 million passengers and one million tonnes of cargo a year. The official Civil Aviation Authority of China (CAAC) plans call for Baiyun to serve as southern China's undisputed domestic aviation hub, with Shenzhen's (which sits just right next to Hong Kong) Huangtian International Airport and the largely unused Zhuhai Airport (just a couple of hours by ferry from Hong Kong) relegated to the status of branch airports.

The threat to Hong Kong from these Mainland airport developments lies in the fact that the Guangdong area, particular the Pearl Delta, accounts for much of the air cargo goods flowing through Hong Kong. Thus, the territory has much to lose if and when cargo firms start operating directly through the Mainland airports. The air transport industry contributes about HK$30 billion to Hong Kong's economy, or 2.5% of GDP. Of the 1.6 million tonnes of cargo that passed through the Hongkong Air Cargo Terminal Ltd. in 2001, more than 90% originated from or were destined for Chinese sources. On the trade side, about 85% of all goods leaving Hong Kong were reexports and about 40% originated from southern China. Although precise data for the share of reexport trade by air is unavailable, it is imaginable that rising competition from Chinese airports would hurt the city's reexport business.

Given their rapid development and government support, it will not be surprising if Baiyun and Shenzhen take over as the regional transport hub if Hong Kong does not liberalise, add value to, and reinvent its facilities fast enough. Multinational logistics companies, like the US FedEx, have already established an operation hub in Shenzhen, allowing some of its traffic to bypass Hong Kong's Chek Lap Kok Airport. This trend will accelerate as cheaper and modernising Chinese facilities race ahead aggressively amid Asia's restructuring process.

China has also been taking steps to open up her air services industry. An agreement signed in 1999 between Beijing and Washington called for the doubling of scheduled flights between each country's carriers to 54 a week. US carriers are free to choose their city of origin and cargo carriers may service any Mainland city, thus reducing the importance of Hong Kong in the air transport chain. US airlines have also an unlimited right to compete with Chinese airlines to fly to regional destinations beyond China on so-called "fifth freedom" services. As of 2002, four US carriers – United Airlines, Northwest Airlines, FedEx, and United Parcel Service (UPS) – are allowed to service Chinese routes.

In the short term, these threats to Hong Kong are contained. This is because the city still has a large amount of intellectual capital with regard to trade and trade facilitation, and there is still more freedom above Hong Kong's sky than China's. While China's air services regime has been liberalised on paper, practical difficulties remain. Beijing has a policy of protecting its growing airline industry and, as a result, foreign carriers do not have access to landing slots at airports. Nor are they allocated frequent take-off slots to build viable services. As Charles Adams, President of UPS (Asia Pacific), pointed out in an interview in March 2002, foreign carriers could fly to China and have unlimited fifth-freedom rights out of China, but they could not fly into China frequent enough. And the frequency will not be available to foreign carriers until the Chinese carriers are assured they can compete with foreign flights on an equal footing. There is also the political argument that there is no reason why Beijing does not want Hong Kong to thrive, and thus it would not allow rampant competition to kill the territory's economic life, at least in the short term.

Nevertheless, this does not deny the longer-term outlook that direct trade and investment between China and the rest of the world underscores the Chinese threat to marginalise Hong Kong's middleman role. As far as the transport and logistics issue goes, Hong Kong lags in the development of air services and modern intermodal links with southern China to exploit any potential synergies and economies of scale. It needs increased access to Chinese destinations if there is to be assurance of continued benefits from the Mainland's economic growth. Fundamentally, Hong Kong is under imminent pressure to reinvent itself as a provider of high valued-added services, presumably in areas such as marketing, banking and insurance, legal and foreign exchange transactions, to survive the China challenge.

Surviving the Challenges

An improvement in the external economic environment will certainly help Hong Kong's cyclical recovery by boosting its exports. China's financial liberalisation measures to allow Mainland investors to buy Hong Kong stocks will help boost local share prices. A stronger stock market will in turn help elevate Hong Kong's private spending via the positive wealth effect – when people feel better and richer, they increase their spending. Indeed, Hong Kong exhibits a much stronger wealth effect than many other economies, even the US. The movement of local stock prices has a strong and positive correlation with retail sales growth. What's more, the time lag between the rise (or fall) in share prices feeding through to a rise (or fall) in retail sales has been short, about one month in Hong Kong compared to much longer lags in other economies. But these cyclical improvements will not solve Hong Kong's structural problems, which are key to the confidence crisis.

Hong Kong must look pass its gloom and develop surviving strategies. It needs to integrate more closely with the Pearl River Delta hinterland so that low value-added production can move to low-cost centres to compete in international markets. A niche area for Hong Kong to ride on China's increasing global trade is logistics – a mix of transport, distribution, supply chain management, and IT. China's entry into the WTO, which will significantly increase foreign trade flows, and her still rudimentary logistics framework have heightened the potential of this sector for the city. Hong Kong must also realign its role in finance to focus on even higher value-added services, notably wealth management, to capture Asia's, particularly China's, rising wealth and savings. Indeed, finance remains one robust area that Hong Kong could continue to excel in, despite rising competition from Shanghai (and to some extent Shenzhen). Hong Kong should also strive to be a platform for interchanges between its powerful neighbours. There is a lot it can learn from Switzerland in this regard.

Hong Kong shares many similar traits with Switzerland. Both are financial capitals, with Hong Kong in capital markets for Asia and Switzerland in private banking for global wealth. Both have built premium services industries, charging high prices for value-added services. While people have complained about Hong Kong's high cost of business and living relative to its neighbours in China, so is Switzerland to many of her European cousins. Both have currencies that make investors worry about their sustainability; Hong Kong's simultaneous currency pegs to the US dollar and the Chinese renminbi and Switzerland's independent Swiss Franc within an integrated European community that uses a common currency, the Euro. Politically, both are situated in some sort of no-man's land, with Hong Kong being both inside and outside of China while Switzerland being in Europe but outside the Euroland.

Since Switzerland remains a premier city in the face of powerful neighbours, and she has developed more fully economically and financially than Hong Kong, there is no reason why Hong Kong cannot replicate the Swiss experience. The key is vision and leadership, which Hong Kong still lacks. Switzerland realises that her small size is a handicap in competing with her neighbours in most areas. She has chosen to build a high-cost, high-living-standard economy on a group of niche industries, such as private banking, luxurious watch-making, pharmaceutical, and up-market food industry. Specialisation has made Swiss companies world experts in each area. This is precisely what Hong Kong has to do to step out of China's economic shadow, as it is too small and too expensive to do everything. Fundamentally, this means that Hong Kong has to revamp its business model from the conventional asset trading and manufacturing practices to brand building and high-value tertiary production.

Viewed from this angle, it is ridiculous to see Hong Kong maintaining her inward-looking measures to keep its old model by continuing to seal its borders from Chinese competition. Despite government efforts, such a policy stands no chance of success. Opening up will bring long-term benefits. Just look at Switzerland. The Swiss have fluid borders with her neighbours. A relatively open border policy has enabled Switzerland to import labour from Austria to the east, Italy to the south, France to the west, and Germany to the north. Benefits are felt on both sides of these borders. Swiss companies are able to cut labour cost and diversify their labour skill base, while neighbouring economies receive boosts from income earned overseas. The Swiss also go to Italy, France, and Germany for shopping much the same way as Hong Kongers travelling to Shenzhen and other southern China cities for weekends. Switzerland is doing all this across national borders in cities that have different cultures and languages. Is it then not myopic for the Hong Kong government to restrict capital and commodity flows between the city and the Mainland, denying it an opportunity to revive?

Developing computer software and services, such as building and maintaining systems for customers, is another possible structural solution. China is fast becoming the manufacturing base for technology equipment, and some Chinese technology companies want to develop indigenous products that rival global giants like Nokia or Cisco. Merely being assemblers of imported components has limited value-add because the assembled products contain specific and often expensive components dictated by foreign manufacturers. This leaves little room for enhancing profits. But if Chinese manufacturers can integrate software design and services in the products, that will allow them greater choice over component purchasing, enhance their bargaining power and add value to raise pricing power.

Providing software to Chinese manufacturers fits Hong Kong's operating environment, as software margins are high but fixed cost is low. But Hong Kong must move fast because India, armed with an ample supply of software engineers, is filling the needs of many Chinese manufacturers. For example, Huawei Technologies, a major communications equipment company with an ambition to become the next Cisco, is cooperating with Indian companies to integrate Indian software with Chinese products. Hong Kong should have an edge over India in working with China because Hong Kong has a lower cultural and language barrier. Cooperation also needs trust and dialogue, which often come from commercial relationships. But China and India do not trade much, with India accounting for only 1% of China's global trade. On the other hand, almost 90% of Hong Kong's exports are reexport trade with China. The Hong Kong government can well spend some of its huge fiscal reserves to improve the basic infrastructure for developing IT platforms, facilitate information and human capital flows, and produce more software engineers to jump-start Hong Kong's knowledge-based industry.

To revamp the corporate sector, the Hong Kong government should provide a sound regulatory and structural framework to improve corporate governance. Companies should establish compensation, audit and governance committees, and have independent directors chairing these committees to improve management transparency and accountability. The independent directors should also comprise a majority of the committee's membership. In North America and Europe, some corporate boards forbid their executives from sitting on more than two other boards and retain the right to veto the companies they join. Hong Kong and other Asian economies should consider adopting this system. It ensures that directors do not spread themselves too thin so that they can fulfill their fiduciary and regulatory duties properly.

All this is easier said than done because of the cosy relationship between government and business in Hong Kong. Chief Executive Tung Chee Wah, who was a business magnate before his official appointment and still maintains close relationship with the local business tycoons, typifies this relationship. It is notable that Tung gives in to pressures from his tycoon friends and compromises his policy from time to time. The endless policy reviews that take place – by the Securities and Futures Commission, the Standing Committee on Company Law Reform and a variety of non-statutory bodies – have not led to any changes. They are just an example of Hong Kong's system failure, where bureaucrats have consultations but no action! Until Hong Kong restructures to allow greater corporate disclosure and transparency, it risks being left behind in the quest for better corporate governance in Asia and thus losing precious long-term foreign investment.

Crucially, the government's attitude has to change to address system failure, which goes a long way to hurt investor confidence. Switzerland's experience shows that an effective government that is in touch with the people is key to drive economic prosperity. The unique Swiss democracy, in which even the smallest proposal requires a majority vote, ensures that the people feel in control of their society. This is in sharp contrast to Hong Kong, where the government has been seen as completely out of touch with the people. Local surveys show that the public is feeling increasingly powerless over their economic and daily affairs. This is not to say Hong Kong has to follow the Swiss political model; indeed, such a model could backfire if too much democracy hinders progress, as everything has to be decided by consensus. But the point is that the government needs to ensure that it has its finger on the pulse of society so that the people can be assured it is committed to their well-being.

Given the ineffective government and its lack of vision and determination, many foreign portfolio investors have made no secret that their enthusiasm for Hong Kong assets is as transient as a love affair. They see Beijing as shrewd, focused, and determined (sometimes ruthless). Hong Kong's leadership is kind and well-meaning but its bloated bureaucracy has all the arrogance of the unaccountable and the intellectual mediocrity of the sinecure. The experience of a fund manager from London who visited Hong Kong in mid-2002 illustrates this problem vividly. He contrasted the HKMA with the Reserve Bank of New Zealand, whose retired governor Don Brash always answered his phone calls and the callers' questions directly. When this London fund manager requested a meeting with the HKMA, they wrote back asking to have the questions submitted ahead of the meeting. After complying with the request, our British friend received a written reply that answered none of his queries. At the end of the reply, the lordships at the HKMA's ivory tower declined to meet up because they claimed they had already answered the questions. This is no way to run a corner shop, not to mention a world-class financial city. This is definitely not the way to attract long-term capital to the Oriental Pearl.

Closed economies afford their planners latitude to make mistakes without suffering much consequences. But an open financial centre, like Hong Kong, leaves little scope for the dead hand of government, lest capital departs elsewhere. Reestablishing predictable and credible rules of the game is key for Hong Kong to rejuvenate itself. The challenging tasks facing the territory underscore precisely the massive competitive pressure stemming from China in the years to come.

Chapter 7

Case Study 2 – China's Pressure on Taiwan

Until the turn of the millennium, Taiwan had been in denial of her structural woes. Whenever economic stress mounted, the Taiwanese government resorted to macroeconomic bailout policies – cutting interest rates, increasing money supply, and raising fiscal spending – and administrative measures, such as capital controls, to salvage the economy. These bailout policies worked well to cover up the island's structural problems, notably a rotten financial system and an overstretched real estate sector, for over three decades. Their success also allowed Taiwan to escape the 1997/1998 Asian crisis almost unscathed, while nearly all other Asian economies were thrown into chaos. Many observers believe that Taiwan's economic success was a result of her good fundamentals. They include a high savings rate, a persistent current account surplus, huge foreign exchange reserves, absence of foreign debt, and a flexible economy dominated by small- and medium-sized firms.

However, Taiwan's economic superiority did not last long, as her lesser-known structural woes started to surface in 2000 when the global economy entered a synchronised slowdown. On the surface, Taiwan was hit hard by sagging global demand, especially electronics products, as the economy went through in 2001 the worst contraction in 50 years. Many locals and foreigners have remained optimistic that Taiwan's economy would recover rapidly from her economic woes along with another upturn in the world's economic cycle. They will be disappointed! It is true that Taiwan has fewer structural problems than many other Asian economies. But this does not mean that she can get away with reform denials forever. The government's bailout to let Taiwan escape from the Asian crisis may be the last trick it could pull off. The rise of China's competitive pressure will be a dominant force aggravating Taiwan's structural stress and dragging her economic growth in the new economic paradigm.

Liquidity Trap is Not the Worst Problem

While a cyclical recovery will raise Taiwan's headline economic growth rate, the optimism for a global upturn lifting Taiwan out of her structural woes is well misplaced. It has become clear that Taiwan's economic woes are deeper than a mere cyclical downturn would suggest. The island's biggest economic challenge, especially after her entry into the WTO in early 2002, is an economic transition under the weight of structural rigidities and rising competition from China. Sustainable economic and asset price growth will depend on whether Taiwan can reinvent herself under an intensifying process of investment and manufacturing hollowing-out to China.

Like Hong Kong's economy (see Chapter 6), Taiwan's economy fell into a liquidity trap, where ample liquidity and record low interest rates had failed to revive economic growth, as it entered the new millennium. Consumer price growth was feeble, falling steadily from an average of 1.2% year-over-year in 2000 to outright deflation (that is negative growth) in 2001 and 2002. The same trend was seen in bank lending, which fell from double-digit growth rates in 2000 to negative growth rates in the following two years. All this happened despite numerous interest rate cuts by the Central Bank of China (CBC) (Taiwan's central bank) since December 2000, which brought the price of credit down to record low levels. The problem with using monetary policy to boost economic growth lied partly in deflation. Although the CBC's massive monetary easing had brought nominal (i.e., not adjusted for inflation) short-term interest rates down by two-and-a-half percentage points by early 2002, price deflation had limited the fall in real (inflation-adjusted) interest rates to only half a percentage point. Taiwan's monetary policy had lost effectiveness in a deflationary environment, where nominal interest rate cuts failed to alter the real cost of capital and, thus, were unable to boost economic growth.

But a liquidity trap may not be the worst problem for Taiwan going forward. Deep structural woes will test investor patience even after the economic cycle recovers. Like Japan, Taiwan has been pursuing macroeconomic bailouts without serious reforms since the 1980s. This can be seen in the sharp rise in public sector borrowing, as summarised by the public debt-to-GDP ratio. The increase in this ratio measures the speed of the government's debt build-up in the economy. Also, the higher the ratio, the heavier the debt burden on the economy. Taiwan's ratio has risen from a low of 4% of GDP in the mid-1980s to over 20% in 2001. Although this debt ratio remains moderate by international standards, the lack of reform coupled with active government bailouts suggest unwillingness on the part of the authorities to let market forces purge the economic imbalances.

Without eliminating economic excess in the system, structural flaws have built up for more than two decades. These woes have blunted the ability of monetary policy to boost growth during periods of economic downturn by impairing the function of the banking system and hurting public confidence. They are manifested in the fall of the banks' ability and appetite to lend and the public's willingness to spend. The crux of the problem lies in the decline of the so-called money velocity, which is simply the number of times that money changes hands. A lower money velocity means that each unit of money is generating a fewer number of transactions, thus dragging economic growth. On the contrary, a higher money velocity generates more transactions and boosts growth. The loss of public confidence has prompted many Taiwanese to curb spending, thus reducing money velocity. Indeed, Taiwan's money velocity has been falling steadily since the 1980s.

Taiwan's prolonged decline in money velocity destroys the effectiveness of monetary expansion in the economy. To consider the problem, observe the following economic logic. From a monetary angle, an economy's output is simply the product of money stock and velocity. When money supply rises (or interest rates fall), even if money velocity stays constant, business transactions still increase, as the rise in money supply (or cut in interest rates) raises demand. On the other hand, at any given level of money supply (or interest rate), when money velocity rises, economic activity rises. In economics, this is summarised by the so-called Quantity Theory of Money, where money stock (M) times velocity (V) equals nominal output (PY), or MV=PY. It is obvious from this simple logic that falling velocity, which reduces economic activity, could offset the impact of a rise in money supply (or a fall in interest rates) on economic output. In other words, no matter how low interest rates go, if the public does not spend or borrow, money velocity still drops and private demand is trapped in dead water. Indeed, this has been a common phenomenon in Taiwan and many other Asian economies after the Asian crisis.

The accumulation of structural flaws in Taiwan's system has resulted in diminishing returns on capital, a dysfunctional banking system, deteriorating debt dynamics, and worsening fiscal balances. Indeed, Taiwan's industries have been suffering from diminishing returns for many years, as industrial output per unit of investment has dropped steadily from a ratio of over 2.5 in the mid-1980s to less than 1.4. This estimation of diminishing investment returns is based on national data provided by the CEIC data bank. This dramatic drop in Taiwan's investment efficiency has been steady and prolonged, as is evident in Figure 7.1. The problem is further worsened by industrial concentration in sectors where price deflation is the most serious, notably manufacturing and electronics products, since the Asian crisis.

Manufacturing is still a big part of Taiwan's economy. Notably, the electronics segment accounts for over one-third of Taiwan's manufacturing industry. But the whole manufacturing sector is suffering from a serious erosion of pricing power and loss of market share as a result of rising competition. China's rapid development into new industries has raised her export penetration to world markets, intensifying competitive pressures and dragging down tradable goods prices globally. This has, in turn, depressed global export prices and created a negative terms-of-trade shock in Taiwan. A fall in the terms of trade means that

Figure 7.1   Falling Returns on Investment

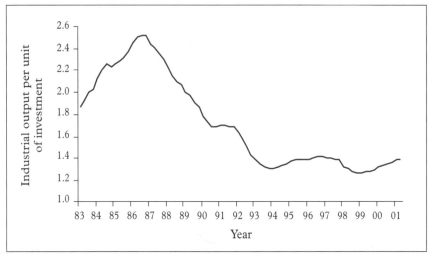

each unit of Taiwanese export could buy less imports, or the Taiwanese had to pay more export dollars to buy any given amount of imports. This is equivalent to a reduction in domestic income and a cut in domestic spending power. The fall in export prices also exerts a profit squeeze on Taiwan's export manufacturers, especially given their high domestic cost base. This in turn hurts corporate earnings growth. China's rising competitive power will intensify the overall negative terms-of-trade impact on Taiwan and inflict significant economic pains on the island's economic transformation process in the new paradigm.

Bad Banks and Debt Trap

Aggravating Taiwan's corporate structural woes is a corrupted domestic financial system, with bad banks struggling in an overcrowded industry. Due to the authorities' bailout policy, Taiwanese banks have not gone through a cleansing process despite retrenchment pressure from the Asian crisis. The island is significantly over-banked, with 23 million people being swamped by more than 50 banks and over 200 credit cooperatives. Further, 13 government-controlled banks have a combined market share of 55%, leaving the remaining banks with tiny market shares of 1% or 2% or less. The government has been able to sustain the weak financial institutions due partly to the lack of foreign debt exposure and partly to foreign exchange controls. Both factors help reduce the potential problem of massive capital withdrawal by foreign creditors. Without foreign debt, there is no risk of foreign lenders calling in loans or not renewing loans to Taiwan when they are due. Foreign exchange controls obviously curb capital outflow without government approval. Further, these factors also lock up domestic liquidity, making it available to the authorities' economic bailout to cushion local financial stress.

Nevertheless, just as it is impossible to wrap fire with paper, Taipei's wholesale economic bailout will not be able to contain economic woes forever. Since the Asian crisis, Taiwan's financial stress has been mounting on the back of deflation. Continued price erosion has destroyed wealth, jobs, and public confidence. As a result, nominal GDP has fallen from near 10% growth rates before the regional debacle to negative growth as the economy enters the new millennium. The economic malaise has also manifested itself in mounting stress in the banking system, with non-performing loans surging from less than 2% of total loan assets in the early 1990s to double-digit percentages by 2002.

Taiwan's banking industry indeed exhibits symptoms similar to the Japanese banking problems. While official data put Taiwan's non-performing loan ratio at the end of 2001 at about 8% of total loans, slightly higher than Japan's 7%, the true bad debt ratio is likely to be at least double the official figures in both economies due to the problem of under-reporting by banks. More alarming is the Taiwanese banks' rapid rate of bad debt accumulation, which had quadrupled, even according to the official data, to 8% in 2001 from just 2% in 1995.

It is almost impossible to estimate Taiwan's true extent of bad loans. This is because there is an underground financial system on the island, which channels millions of dollars of funds from the official system (banks and cooperatives) to speculators in the asset market. The problem dated back to the mid-1980s and early 1990s, when the CBC's massive monetary easing prompted a bank-lending binge and an asset bubble. More than a decade of aggressive expansion at the expense of lending prudence and high loan concentration in the property sector have stranded many Taiwanese banks with poor asset quality and credit risk. This structural stress was intensified by poor economic conditions during the global economic slowdown in 2001 and 2002, as seen in the banks' rising loan loss provisions and declining loan loss coverage. When the amount of loans covered by loss reserves falls, bank asset quality suffers. Taiwanese banks' loan loss provisions have been rising since the mid-1990s at an average annual rate of 15%. And their asset quality, as measured by the loan loss coverage (calculated as the ratio of loss reserves to gross loans), has also been worsening. Taiwan's loan loss coverage has never recovered to its high levels seen before 1990.

Central to the financial flaws is the triangle relationship between the legal banking institutions, the illegal financial system, and the asset market. Sharp drops in local asset prices have exposed this unhealthy relationship. Banks lend a lot of money to stock and property punters via the underground system. This practice creates a problem as the value of this type of bank asset is tied to the fortune of the stock and real estate markets. Although official data for bank lending to stock and property speculation are unavailable, a proxy can be found in the bank loans to personal business investment. According to the central bank's data, this category is an aggregate for all types of business investments by individuals, like manufacturing, retail, real estate, and portfolio investment. The growth of these bank loans to personal investments explains, with statistical significance, almost half of the growth in margin transactions of listed stocks in Taiwan. The point is that a stock market crash creates an ugly knock-on effect by hurting the underground financial system, which in turn hurts the banking system.

The political ownership structure of the banking system is the biggest structural flaw. This is because it creates a conflict of interest with the government being both the regulator and the regulated in many cases. The local financial institutions are mostly controlled or majority-owned by powerful politicians, especially from the largest political party, the Kuomintang (KMT). This has resulted in both capital forbearance and poor regulatory controls. Since politicians who control the depository institutions also have close investment ties to the asset market, they have a strong incentive to support asset prices and tend to ignore the woes of the underground financial system. This also explains why Taipei has never had the will to purge financial excesses in the system.

Hence, despite robust economic growth between 1995 and 1998, Taiwan's non-performing loans continue to surge. This is strong evidence that there was more to financial system problems than cyclical fluctuations could explain. When strong growth does not reduce bad loans, the underlying problems are obviously structural in nature. With rising competition and persistent deflation dominating the new economic paradigm and the advent of China's entry into the global production stage, Taiwan's economy is unlikely to grow as robust as the 6% average annual rate in the mid-1990s. Inherent structural fractures will continue to haunt the economy.

With the change of political power in 2000, when the opposition Democratic Progressive Party (DPP) defeated the long-ruling KMT in the presidential election, the new DPP government has taken a bolder attitude to face the island's structural woes. In mid-2002, Taiwan took some of its first steps towards banking reform to create fewer but healthier banks. Some of the island's main financial services groups also announced plans to merge with or acquire domestic banks and securities firms. Some banks announced bad-debt write-offs or agreed to sell problem loans to foreign and local investors that specialise in debt recovery. For example, the government-controlled United World Commercial Bank disposed US$514 million worth of bad loans through sales and write-offs. This deal followed an unprecedented sale by the government-owned First Commercial Bank, Taiwan's fourth largest bank, of non-performing loans in early 2002 to debt-recovery specialists.

The decision to dispose bad debts is a dramatic change in Taiwan's banking industry. The financial pressure has finally forced Taiwanese banks to search for a new financial architecture to cut costs and achieve economies of scale to survive the Chinese challenge and rising competition. Taipei has begun building the foundation for bank consolidation since 2000. New laws offer tax breaks and other incentives for mergers and acquisitions. The Financial Holding Company Act, enacted in 2001, has paved the way for existing financial companies to establish 14 new groups that have larger stock market capitalisations and can make more efficient use of their subsidiaries' capital. Bank bad-debt write-off auctions are catching international attention too, with foreign investment houses such as Goldman Sachs, Leman Brothers, and Lone Star Fund of the US expressing keen interest in buying Taiwanese distressed debts.

Taipei has also taken the initiative to create asset management companies (AMCs), which aim at using government funds to buy questionable loans from banks, group them into asset pools, and then sell these pools as bonds to investors. If implemented properly, these AMCs will purge the bad loans on bank balance sheets and thereby free the banks to engage in new lending. This approach will go a long way to bringing Taiwanese banks back to health and giving them the ability to finance economic expansion. An AMC solution should also have other long-term constructive benefits for Taiwan. The pool of bank loans for sale as bonds in the open market should contribute to the development of a broader corporate bond market in Taiwan. In time, such a market would relieve the economy of its over-reliance on bank financing. Not only would the alternative financial channels offer flexibility to Taiwanese business funding needs, broadened financial markets would also offer the island some protection against a future financial crisis.

Nevertheless, it remains to be seen how serious Taipei will push structural reforms. So far, corporate reforms have been quiet. The AMC solution could be stuck in dead water, ā la Japan, and mergers and acquisitions could create bigger dinosaurs if not implemented properly. Even if Taiwan's banks escaped the Asian crisis shock, many of them have continued their imprudent lending practices, making unsound loans. Thus, while some banks are writing-off existing bad loans, others are still piling them up. Some banks are so riddled with bad loans that should simply be shut down, but the government seems to remain tolerant. Do not underestimate the power of the resistance to reform. Many vested interests stand to lose out, whether as shareholders of soon-to-be defunct banks or as parties behind the dubious lending activities. They have voices in the Legislature, which has the power to approve and block reform bills. Hence, there is doubt as to how fast Taipei can change its reform attitude after decades of forbearance and bailouts. After all, the island has very little foreign debt such that it is not subject to foreign creditors' discipline to change, and it is still rich enough to fend off any imminent domestic financial crisis by pumping money into the system.

In addition to banking woes, deteriorating debt dynamics have further deepened Taiwan's financial fault line. While the island has little foreign debt, it suffers from a large domestic (private) debt overhang, which amounts to over 170% of GDP – one of the highest ratios in Asia. This huge domestic debt load has become a serious problem as Taiwan's nominal GDP growth rate has slipped below nominal interest rates. For example, while the local prime rate has remained above 7% a year since the Asian crisis, nominal GDP has slipped from a growth rate of almost 9% a year in early 1998 to a contraction rate of more than 2% in 2001.

When nominal growth is lower than nominal interest rates, the debt dynamics become vicious. This is because when total income is not enough to cover interest payments, servicing the existing debt needs additional borrowing, thus snowballing the debt stock and siphoning more resources from productive use. Deflation is the main culprit that causes the contraction of nominal GDP. As a result, the gap between nominal interest rates and nominal growth in Taiwan could persist, as deflationary pressure remains strong under the shadow of China's competitive threat in the coming years. Meanwhile, the combination of debt deflation could cause major economic disruptions and drag on the local economy and financial markets for years.

The China factor could worsen Taiwan's deflationary process; a defining characteristic of Japan's long economic stagnation. Indeed, the combination of local structural woes and external China stress could push Taiwan into a Japanese-style, debt-deflation quagmire. Under a high bad debt burden, Japanese banks have been unwilling and unable to lend since the 1990s. The lack of credit growth has exacerbated Japan's weak domestic investment and poor consumer demand, and in turn worsened deflation. The combination of soft demand and the lack of pricing power has crimped Japanese corporate earnings and raised the debt burden, contributing to more non-performing loans. All of these have also happened in Taiwan, although to a lesser extent for the time being. Thus, Taiwan's declining bank loan growth throughout the 1990s is unlikely to rebound anytime soon due to the same reasons of intensifying bad debt burden and worsening debt dynamics.

Like Japan, Taiwan is vulnerable to banking problems. This is because she has yet to develop a deep commercial paper market and a substantial corporate bond market to offer business borrowers an alternative to bank financing. That means all financial risks are concentrated in the banks, with no capital market to reduce the systemic risk. The economic environment under WTO will be tougher, with competitive and deflationary pressures intensifying as financial liberalisation picks up steam under WTO requirements. With crippled banks and no viable alternative financial channels, Japan has stagnated. The odds are high that Taiwan could follow suit.

Rubbing Salt into the Wound

Adding to these woes is Taiwan's chronic budget deficit, which has become more than a cyclical concern. Normally, the fiscal deficit should fall or even turn into a surplus during an economic upturn, as government spending on welfare and other needs to boost growth falls while fiscal revenues rise on increasing income and business activities. However, Taipei's fiscal book has not improved even during economic booms. The central government's budget deficit has risen to over 4% of GDP from 2% in 1991, while the combined provincial and central fiscal deficit is over 6% of GDP. The central and provincial governments' combined budget had not seen a fiscal surplus throughout the 1990s, despite strong growth in the early and mid-1990s. According to international experience, a fiscal deficit of over 3% of GDP is unsustainable. It will lead to major economic problems later, as the government draws away private sector resources via borrowing or raises taxes to close the deficit. These measures will crowd out private capital, push up interest rates, and reduce private sector demand and investment.

The deficit becomes more worrying if Taipei's contingent liability in the banking system is taken into account. The official estimate of the bad debt ratio stood at about 8% of total bank loans (or 12% of GDP) in 2001, while private sector estimates put the ratio at at least twice the official figure. Even if Taipei were to bailout only half of the bad debts, it would mean spending an amount equivalent to 10% of total economic output (or US$30 billion). This will certainly add significantly to the fiscal spending and cause the budget deficit to explode. The outlook for balancing the budget in the medium term is dim because Taipei's rising spending to boost GDP growth and the potential loss of fiscal revenues resulting from local businesses hollowing-out to China will continue.

However, Taiwan's fiscal woes may not explode in the short term, given the high private sector savings, which amounts to 26% of GDP, and strong public sector borrowing ability. Despite high private sector debt, total government debt is still less than 30% of GDP, far below the 60% safety threshold deemed by the international community. Do not bet on a financial blowout either, despite the large financial stress. Like Hong Kong, Taiwan is also a net foreign creditor while the crisis-hit countries (South Korea, Thailand, and Indonesia), who suffered a financial collapse, were all big net foreign debtors. Taiwan's gross foreign debt amounts to less than 18% of GDP, compared to over 60% in the crisis-hit countries before the 1997/1998 regional crisis. This means that Taiwan is not under the threat of massive withdrawal by foreign creditors. Even if all foreign creditors wanted to pull out, Taiwan's US$130 billion strong foreign reserves are over twice her foreign debts.

Taiwan's persistent current account surplus (averaging 2% of GDP) and huge foreign reserves (over 40% of GDP) are also in marked contrast to the large current account deficits and dwindling foreign reserves in the crisis-hit countries before the regional debacle. Crucially, Taiwan's financial market is much less open than many of her Asian counterparts. Foreign participation in the Taiwanese bourse accounts for less than 10% of total market capitalisation. The government's Qualified Foreign Institutional Investors (QFII) guidelines also impose strict controls on portfolio flows and foreign investment in local equities. Coupled with capital controls, all this limits the damage of hot money flows into the local system. Thus, the island is not susceptible to a sudden reversal of foreign creditor/investor funds, which was the trigger that set off the Asian financial meltdown in 1997/1998.

The China Squeeze

However, compared to other Asian economies' financial and structural problems, Taiwan's woes are aggravated by an economic transition which threatens a significant hollowing-out of the manufacturing sector to China. This hollowing out process, which began in the 1980s, is in fact an attempt by Taiwan businesses to survive by relocating to the cheaper Mainland. The Chinese pressure can notably be felt in Taiwan's life after her WTO entry, as trade liberalisation will bring some significant short-term economic pains due to rising competition, especially from China. Taiwan's bans on direct trade and investment links with China have shielded the local agricultural sector, the auto industry, and many low- to medium-end manufacturers from Chinese competition for years.

The eventual scrapping of the bans will force a shakeout in Taiwan's sunset industries. Even the textile industry, which has been downsizing steadily since 1980s, may have to retrench further. This is because restructuring of the textile industry so far has mainly involved shifting downstream industries to the Mainland. The remaining local production is still protected. But China's product quality is catching up fast. Persistent excess capacity in China's upstream industries is also emitting deflationary pressure and squeezing profits. Thus, freer trade under the WTO will only lead to further retrenchment of Taiwan's textile sector.

The potential industrial shakeout will also force more local companies, including those in the strong electronics sector, to relocate to China for survival. China is becoming the investment hub for the electronics industry, attracting significant investment from foreign giants like IBM, Intel, Motorola, and NEC. In 2000, Chinese President Jiang Zemin's son teamed up with the son of one of Taiwan's richest tycoon to set up a US$1.6 billion chip plant near Shanghai. This "silicon rush" into China will speed up Taiwan's investment migration to the Mainland in the new economic paradigm.

Industrial shakeout and investment hollowing-out in the coming years will hurt Taiwan's economy and cost more jobs. The official Council for Economic Planning and Development estimated that even a smooth WTO accession would flip Taiwan's trade surplus into a deficit of US$5.3 billion within a short period of time and cost at least 20,000 jobs. But this is an economic cost that Taiwan will have to pay to survive in an increasingly competitive world. With electronics and technology-related products, which are Taiwan's industrial lifeline, being commoditised rapidly, whoever can produce these goods at the lowest cost will survive. "Commoditisation" of the electronics industry refers to the process in which production is increasingly transparent and competition is increasingly cutthroat so that profit margins are being eliminated. Thus, economic integration with China gives Taiwanese manufacturers a chance to survive by relocating to a cheaper Chinese production base and tapping the vast potential of the Mainland market. The explosive surge in Taiwan's exports to China highlights the island's intensifying outsourcing strategy, as parts are shipped to China to be processed, assembled, and reexported to the world market.

Under these pressures, Taiwan's economic future may mirror Hong Kong's industrial development, as the urgency to outsource production is rising. Hong Kong manufacturers moved their production to southern China in the 1980s to escape high local production costs. The whole manufacturing base was relocated to the Mainland within a decade, leaving only the high value-added segments, such as logistics and marketing, in the territory. Such economic retrenchment has shrunk Hong Kong's manufacturing employment sharply to 9% of total employment from over 22% in the early 1990s. However, as evident in the data depicted by Figure 7.2, the share of employment in Taiwan's manufacturing sector has remained relatively stable at around 30%. This suggests that Taiwan's manufacturing employment had not gone through any major shake-up. But as the hollowing-out process to China intensifies, the island's manufacturing employment will likely face a similar fate as Hong

Figure 7.2   Share of Maunfacturing Employment

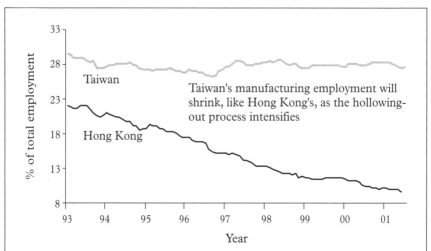

Kong. The Taiwanese economy will evolve into a more service-based system, with the pace of evolvement accelerating under the economic pressure from China.

Thus, a large part of Taiwan's economic transformation in the new paradigm involves integration with the Mainland's economy. This process may be painful, but it is inevitable. Politics, with regard to the unification with China, may be prohibitive. But most Taiwanese businessmen, especially those who have invested millions in the Mainland, are strongly against any moves towards political independence that will irritate China. Some are sanguine that there would be no possibility of real war, except the war of words between the two sides. These optimists argue that Taiwan and China had two completely different political systems. Compared with China, Taiwan is a freer place where people can voice differing opinions. Thus, politicians say different things in different places, which can easily attract all kinds of speculation. To the optimists, Taiwan President Chen Shui-bian's flammable remarks in August 2002 that Taiwan and China were both independent countries on either side of the Taiwan Strait and his support for a referendum on independence were crying wolf. Although the incident provoked a furious, yet controlled, response from Beijing, including the threat of war and a large scale military practice in

Shanghai against a simulated Taiwan air raid, economic integration on both sides would be crucial enough to avoid military skirmishes.

No one knows for sure how much money Taiwanese companies have invested in China. This is because many go through Hong Kong, the US, the British Virgin Islands, Bermuda and another third country to eschew Taipei's official ban on many investments in the Mainland. Such firms appear in Mainland statistics as foreign investment from those places. Various estimates put the accumulated amount of Taiwanese investment in China at over US$120 billion since the late 1980s. Taiwan local business surveys show that her companies had invested all over China, including provinces that other foreign investors have avoided. Guangdong, Jiangsu, Fujian, Shanghai, and Zhejiang are the most popular spots for Taiwan investment.

When Taiwanese firms began investing in China in the 1980s, they were concentrated in the Pearl River Delta and Fujiang province with low-technology, labour intensive industries. In the early to mid-1990s, they went up-market, turning to Guangdong cities, such as Shenzhen, Dongguan, Shunde, Panyu, and Foshan, as production bases for electronics and computer exports. Since the late 1990s, Taiwanese firms have moved into Shanghai, Kunshan, and Hangzhou, turning those areas into a second production base. Electronics and electrical products account for over half of Taiwan's investment in these three cities, followed by metallurgy and plastics, chemicals, machinery, textiles, transport equipment, and food.

Taiwan also depends heavily on trade with the Mainland, as she exports about US$30 billion worth of goods to China a year. This is equivalent to almost 10% of Taiwan's GDP. And this amount is growing along with the hollowing-out of Taiwan industries to China, as Taiwanese firms on the Mainland buy parts, raw materials, and other intermediate goods from their parent companies. The hollowing-out and economic integration are indeed different modes of the same transformation process. Hollowing-out allows Taiwan businesses to cut production cost via relocation to the Mainland. It also leads to an increase in Taiwan exports to China. Both modes serve to accelerate the economic integration process between the two economies.

Taiwan needs to look for a new economic road. The local cost of labour and land are going up, prices are rising, and the cost of environmental control is escalating. Politicians may not like the giant sucking sound from China, but moving offshore is the only way to survive.

A Secular Downtrend

Cross-strait politics could cause major volatility to Taiwan's economic transition, although Taiwanese authorities seem to have finally realised the inevitability of the island's economic road. Former President Lee Teng-hui's so-called "go-south" policy in 1996 tried to redirect Taiwan investment from China by encouraging Taiwanese businesses to invest in Southeast Asia. It has failed completely, as Taiwanese have kept looking towards China, defying official bans. When Chen Shui-bian came to power in 2000, he decided to change Taipei's strategic policy from avoiding integration with China to active engagement. For example, limits to investment in the Mainland have been relaxed, certain ports are allowed to conduct direct trade with China and Taiwanese financial institutions are allowed to deal directly with Mainland banks. But both sides are still far from arriving at a political resolution surrounding the "One China" policy. Any political stand-off between Taipei and Beijing will complicate Taiwan's economic integration with the Mainland and inflict more pains in her survival under China's rising economic clout.

Politics aside, Taiwan still faces the strategic decision and challenge of replacing her manufacturing sector once it is hollowed-out. A crucial question is whether Taiwan could become a financial centre, with heavy interventionist policies and a shaky banking system. The prospects for this development is dim because with the presence of Hong Kong, Singapore, and the swift ascent of Shanghai as a financial centre, Asia probably does not need another financial hub. Taiwan will then have to consider moving up the value-added ladder by focusing on knowledge-based capital goods. Although this is an area that Taiwan has excelled in, this development will put her in direct and increasing competition with China, Hong Kong, and Singapore who are also moving in the same direction. Given a

Taiwanese system that has been protected for so long, this challenge to confront external giants via the open market will inevitably create uncertainty that could hurt local confidence and a drag on Taiwan's growth and investment for a long time.

Give the amount of reform inertia in the Taiwan system, structural changes are easier said than done. A comparison with another Asian tiger economy, South Korea, shows that Taiwan has been lagging far behind in reinventing her system as it moves into the new paradigm. The notable difference lies in the growth rates between South Korea and Taiwan during the global economic slowdown in 2001 and 2002. Although South Korea still has a lot to do in reforming her economy – she has also cheated on reform – she has done the most among the Asian economies in financial restructuring (see Chapter 2). This is the reason why South Korea was able to grow by an average of 5% during the global economic slowdown while Taiwan suffered her worst economic contraction in 50 years. South Korea's achievement is the strongest evidence of the benefits and ability of structural changes to rejuvenate economic growth.

Korea's success reflects badly on Taiwan's reform deficiency because the two economies share many similarities in their early stages of economic development. Both economies based their industrial policy models on Japan when they began industrialisation in the 1980s. Both graduated from the developing economy status and became industrialised economies in the 1990s by pursuing aggressive export-oriented growth models. They have similar domestic savings rates, per capita income levels and export shares in the economy. Besides these positive developments, the two economies also share many similar economic woes. Both have shaky banking systems, with heavy government meddling in the financial sectors. Both have suffered from excess savings and over investment that created economic bubbles. Their governments have pursued a too-big-to-fail policy for economic bailouts.

Both economies are indeed a derivative of the Japanese economic model, which is driven by exports and production and supported by high savings and investment in the pursuit of market share instead of investment returns. Such a model does not only characterise the Korean and Taiwanese economic development; it also defines Asia's growth model since the 1980s. However, rising Chinese industrial power, intensifying global competition and the persistent fall in tradable prices have made the Japanese-based model redundant. The region's clones of the Japanese model, like Taiwan and Korea, must restructure dramatically to avoid the risk of long-term erosion in productivity, growth and living standards.

However, Korea and Taiwan's economic similarities stopped after the Asian crisis. The challenges in the new economic era require the Asian economies to move away from their export- and production-oriented model and focus on generating domestic growth momentum, like consumption. Korea has led Taiwan by a wide margin in this broad line of restructuring. For example, Korea's exports as a share of industrial output peaked at the time when the Asian crisis broke out. Her ratio of exports-to-industrial output fell steadily from 110% in 1997 to around 85% in 2002, with the rate of decline accelerated sharply since 1999. On the other hand, Taiwan has stuck with the old export-led model, with her export ratio rising from 100% in 1997 to 110% in 2002. As a result, Korea's net export-to-GDP ratio has fallen steadily, while Taiwan's ratio has continued to rise. This is obvious evidence that Korea has aggressively cut export dependence by moving away from export-led growth, while Taiwan has kept the status quo and thus remains at the mercy of external demand changes.

To prompt the needed structural shift in aggregate demand from exports to domestic sources, Korea has moved decisively to raise local consumption. Korea's domestic spending has risen sharply since 2001, where private consumption growth as a share of GDP growth surged from less than 1% to more than 4% a year. Financial liberalisation has helped, as increasing consumer access to mortgage and personal loans has supported booming property and services sectors after the Asian crisis. On the other hand, there has not been any obvious structural rise in the share of consumer spending in Taiwan's economy. Its property and services sectors are still depressed five years after the regional debacle. This divergence in the structural behaviour between the two economies reflects Taiwan's continued heavy reliance on exports and manufacturing and Korea's retreat from them.

Korea's thriving non-tradable sectors on the back of falling tradable goods prices also indicate clearly that she was attempting to re-write its economic model by adopting a new, domestic driven, economic path, while Taiwan was still buried in inertia.

These developments have important repercussions for the two economies in the new economic era. South Korea's reduced export dependency means that the deflationary impact of a strong Korean won would have a less negative impact on her economy than Taiwan's. On the other hand, the continuation of Taiwan's heavy export dependency means that the New Taiwan dollar would have a long-term inherent weakness in the coming deflationary environment. To compete with China and other Asian exporters in the face of feeble external demand (see Chapter 8) and falling prices, Taiwan just cannot afford an expensive currency. Further, Taiwan's high concentration on exports means that domestic price structures are strongly affected by global tradable goods prices, which are being eroded by globalisation and excess capacity. The presence of low-cost producers, notably China, and falling prices suggest that the New Taiwan dollar exchange rate would remain under prolonged downward pressure. Any strengthening of the currency will only hurt exports and pull down economic growth, inflicting more deflationary pains.

In a nutshell, Taiwan's economy could be trapped in a secular downward trend for many years with cyclical upturns in the short and medium term. This means that economic growth and the local financial markets would receive a boost whenever global, especially electronics, demand picks up. But each cyclical peak will likely be lower than the preceding one, giving rise to a succession of declining peaks following a long-term declining trend. This secular declining growth trend is defined by Taiwan's economic transformation under the weight of structural rigidities and rising competitive stress from China. To break out of this negative secular trend, Taiwan will need to overcome the structural and political impasse and rejuvenate herself, like Hong Kong did in the 1980s and early 1990s, to focus on consumption, services, and production where her comparative advantages lie.

Chapter 8

The Big Picture and the New Paradigm

The new economic paradigm of rising competition, disinflation with periodic deflationary traps, profit squeeze, and constrained economic growth is a product of both secular supply and demand imbalances. China is an aggravating factor to these forces. The cost efficiency that Chinese manufacturers have been able to achieve with reforms and economies of scale means that the world would be entering a new era of ample cheap tradable goods. Hence, China's rising economic clout is exerting a big competitive stress on Asian economies, intensifying their inherent excess capacity problem due to accumulated structural woes and insufficient reforms.

Adding to this supply-side deflationary pressure is subdued global demand. Prolonged robust demand growth that existed in the 1990s is unlikely to emerge anytime soon. The global economy is debt-strapped, with consumers over-spent and corporates over-invested via excessive borrowing. Continued erosion of pricing power and profits in the new economic era will hurt confidence, investment, and consumption decisions. To complete our analysis, let us look at the secular forces behind the global demand constraint. We will then discuss Asia's new business model in the new economic paradigm and conclude with a note on China's role in the region's economic transformation.

A Global Problem

The major reason why sustained strong demand is not returning anytime soon is because the global economy is facing a huge debt mountain. At every economy we look, the economic balance sheet is overstretched. This factor will remain a major drag on demand growth for years. In the 1990s, robust global economic conditions, especially in the US, helped Asia rebound quickly, albeit only briefly, from the regional financial crises. So, the feeble global demand outlook is bad news for Asia. The growth problem is especially acute this time because there will be no robust global demand to salvage Asia from its painful post-bubble economic transformation by absorbing Asian exports on the back of excess supply.

Late 2001 and 2002 saw the largest-ever sovereign debt default in Argentina and the biggest-ever corporate bankruptcy of Enron, a giant energy trading company, in the US. The Enron debacle was followed by a series of high profile financial failures by other major US companies, such as WorldCom, America's second largest telecom company, and K-Mart, America's second largest retailer and UAL.Corp, one of the largest airlines in the world. These notable incidences underscore the risk that the heavy debt build-up in the global economy in the 1990s could dampen any robust economic growth. The lack of inflation during the decade means that the real debt burden has been rising, constraining demand growth in the future. The outlook for prolonged disinflation with periods of deflationary traps means that the real debt burden will remain high, with financial stress mounting at times, to weigh on aggregate spending for many years.

The US consumer and corporate sector acquired a huge borrowing appetite in the 1990s and piled up record debts relative to their incomes. Total private sector debt rose at an annual rate of 6% after adjustment for inflation at the end of 2001, despite the US economic recession. This borrowing craze was in sharp contrast to the fall in real private sector debt levels in the past economic slowdown. Americans are not alone in piling up debt. Their European cousins and even the frugal Japanese have been on a similar borrowing binge. For example,

British household debt rose to a record 120% of personal disposable income in 2001 from 100% in 1997. German households' total borrowing amounted to 115% of their income in 2000, up 30 percentage points from 1991. Meanwhile, despite the Japanese reputation of being one of the biggest savers in the world, they are also big borrowers with household debt amounting to over 130% of disposable income in 2000.

The US may be the largest debtor in the world in absolute dollar terms, but she is not the most excessive borrower when debt is measured as a share of disposable income. Some may be surprised that the household sectors in Japan, Germany, and Britain all have a much bigger debt burden than the US. In the decade between 1991 and 2001, total US household debt amounted to an average of 97% of personal disposable income. However, consumers in Germany, Britain, and Japan plunged more into debt. Total household debt averaged 103% of personal disposable income in Germany, 110% in Britain, and a whopping 134% in Japan. Consumers in the major economies were caught in a spend-and-borrow spiral like there was no tomorrow. This explosive borrow-to-spend behaviour is a result of financial maturity. Development in the banking systems in mature economies has enabled consumers to make an intertemporal choice by borrowing future income to finance current consumption. While this may be good news for consumers, their excessive borrowing habit has also impaired their future finances.

Corporate debt has also soared to record levels in the world's major economies. In the US, for example, the ratio of total corporate liabilities to corporate net worth has risen to an average of 109% in recent years from 60% in the 1970s. Indeed, most of the global debt build-up comes from the US. The world's largest economy initiated a global corporate borrowing binge in the early 1980s, thanks to the then junk bond king, Michael Milken, who fundamentally changed the process of debt creation and accumulation. Previously, companies relied on their banks to provide them with capital. Since Michael Milken's revolutionary junk bond success in the early 1980s, they have gone directly to the capital market for funding. As a result, US corporate bond issuance has soared to three times that of corporate bank loans from 1.5 times in the 1970s. What's more, US corporate debt both as a percentage of GDP and of profits have also soared to record levels.

This revolutionary change in corporate finance in the US has spread far beyond the US national borders to other major economies and beyond the corporate sector. Its emergence was due partly to the development of a more efficient financial system that better matches savers with borrowers, and partly to financial deregulation in the late 1970s and early 1980s, which favoured debt accumulation by the private sector. Unfortunately, not all of the borrowing has been used wisely. In the second half of the 1990s, most US corporates issued debt to finance share buy-back programmes or to invest in high-tech sectors. Similarly in Europe, much of corporate borrowing was also linked to high-tech and telecom companies, notably their overly optimistic investment in third generation mobile phone licences. However, such high-tech and telecom investments have turned out to be imprudent decisions based more on hype than fundamentals. The resultant excess capacity will linger for many years, so that capital investment growth in the major economies of Japan, Europe, and America will remain subdued. This will in turn constrain economic growth and adding to deflationary pressure.

The borrowing binge of consumers and corporates means that private sector balance sheets in the world's major economies are overstretched. Their rising debt burden is threatening future growth. Debt is not a problem if it is based on sound spending decisions that put surplus savings to better use by investors with profitable businesses. But in most rich countries, private sector debt has been rising excessively relative to GDP since the Second World War. Crucially, the rapid debt build-up during the 1980s and 1990s in the global economy has created an undesirable by-product. It has fundamentally changed the power structure of credit creation by eroding the effectiveness of monetary policy in the financial system. Conducting monetary policy in a debt-strapped economy with deflation is like pushing a string; one is unable to achieve the defined policy objective, be it controlling inflation or economic growth, as desired. This is because interest rate cuts have become ineffective in boosting private spending (see next section).

Following the burst of the global stock market bubble in 2001, the world economy has to go through a period of post-bubble adjustments. This process involves purging economic and financial excesses via debt reduction, spending retrenchment, and falling asset prices. There has never been a case in history where an economy could escape serious calamity after the bursting of an asset bubble. Just look at the notable examples of the US in the 1930s and early 1970s, Japan in the early 1990s, and, most recently, Asia in 1997/1998. With the exception of the early 1970s, when a severe economic recession rampant inflation caused, all other post-bubble economic tragedies shared some common adjustment characteristics.

The most dramatic malaise is sharp economic recession, or even depression as in the US in the 1930s, following the collapse of asset prices. The economic contraction leads to a structural downward shift in economic growth in the aftermath of the asset bubble bursting. Notably in Japan, pre-bubble growth averaged 4.5% a year; but the post-bubble average has been only 1.1%. Similarly, Asia's average growth rate of 6.5% in the decade before the regional crisis has been halved after the crisis. Another post-bubble characteristic is strong deflationary pressures. General price levels have been falling in Japan since 1994 and in Asia since 1998/1999. What's more, the Asian deflationary tendency has spread to the global economy since 2001. Finally, post-bubble recovery in corporate profits takes a long time. For example, it took the US 15 years after the Great Depression in 1930 to recover corporate profits back to pre-crash levels. Asia's corporate profits have remained compressed since the Asian crisis (see Chapter 2). And odds are high that there would be a long way for Asian profits to climb back to their pre-crisis levels.

It is possible that Asia has entered the new economic paradigm, with China as the major force shaping it, at the same time when the world economy has entered a protracted period of post-bubble adjustments. The combined deflationary forces from Asia and the rest of the world are unprecedented. They will be so huge and protracted that they would surprise and disappoint many, especially those who still think the good old days of fast growth and easy money would return after this adjustment period is over. Given the problem of broken balance sheets in major economies, the global adjustment process will create a hostile macro backdrop for Asia's economic transformation and makes its transition tougher than it would otherwise be. Add in the competitive stress from China, and Asia's post-bubble adjustment could even dwarf the longevity of America's adjustment after the Great Depression in the 1930s.

The Evil Combination

Debt without deflation or deflation with little debt is not a serious problem because macroeconomic policies could rectify the situation easily. It is the evil combination of debt and deflation that could produce major economic problems, including rising unemployment, eroding confidence, and falling economic growth. This is because in a deflationary environment, falling prices raise the real debt burden, thus drawing away more and more resources from productive economic activity to debt servicing. Unfortunately, global demand is facing an evolving debt-deflation environment in the coming years, as the huge global debt load meets a disinflationary environment with periodic deflation traps. Deflationary pressure will remain a dominant force, especially in Asia (thanks to the rising competitive power of China) for a long time. Thus, despite low nominal interest rates, the real debt service burden will remain high or even rise in the rich economies, especially in the US, stifling income and demand growth momentum.

The consequences are negative for demand growth. Inflation is an escape route for debtors, as rising prices erode the real value of their debts. But in the new disinflation/deflation era, debtors can no longer rely on inflation to erode their real debt burden. The process of repairing balance sheets to reduce debt and rebuild wealth and liquidity takes longer as the heavy real debt burden in the absence of inflation will keep siphoning resources away to plug the debt hole. The result is a protracted fall in nominal income. Japan offers a clear example of debt and deflation combined to compress nominal GDP by swelling the real debt burden of both the public and private sectors. The evil combination has trapped the Japanese economy in a recessionary quagmire since the early 1990s.

Without repairing the consumer, corporate, and public sector balance sheets, any demand recovery in the global economy will likely be feeble. Shaky financial health suggests that there would be little room for further borrowing to help pull the global economy out of the doldrums. Rising government budget deficits all over the world are pushing global authorities into the fiscal corner, reducing their ability to boost growth during a cyclical downturn. Thus, when the next down cycle hits, bigger problems will emerge as the pressure to repair balance sheets may intensify the contraction pressure on aggregate spending.

Although, heavy borrowing by rich countries have not resulted in a full-blown crisis like in Argentina and other Latin American economies (and hopefully this will not happen in the new economic era), excessive debt acts as a significant drag on growth that can amplify economic downturns. The painful experience in the early 1990s underscores the evil of excessive debt. The most protracted periods of below-trend growth were found in Britain, Canada, and Sweden because they had built up record amounts of private sector debt in the 1980s. In Asia, the weight of Japan's total (public plus private) debt, amounting to over 150% of GDP, threatens to stifle her growth for many more years. Being the second largest economy in the world, Japan's prolonged economic weakness will only add to the burden of demand deficiency in Asia.

Contrary to the conventional wisdom that monetary reflation can boost demand growth, central banks' ability to push their economies out of the debt trap by monetary expansion is blunted by the lack of inflation. During periods of deflation, monetary easing measures, such as interest rate cuts, are useless. This is because falling prices act to raise real interest rates (as approximated by nominal interest rate minus inflation rate), which are the ultimate variable that affects spending and investment decisions. As the case of Taiwan shows (see Chapter 7), deepening deflation could nullify the authorities' monetary stimulus of nominal interest rate cuts.

In a deflationary environment, monetary easing becomes a race between the pace of nominal interest rate cuts and the rate of price decline. If prices decline faster than that of nominal rate cuts, real interest rates rise so that rate cuts by the central bank are helpless to boost growth. Even worse, global monetary authorities have not yet been able to fully understand the deflation monster, which will haunt the global economy for years. For decades, high inflation was the main source of economic instability. Notably in the 1970s when inflation was rampant, corporate managers acted as if the name of the game was to raise annual sales by acquisitions and mergers, as well as through marketing decisions that included frequent price increases. Managers were paid more as long as they could contribute to growth in company revenues. Little effort was devoted to economic efficiency. The choice for central banks then was accomodating inflation or reducing output and employment growth. Hence, central banks were focusing on fighting inflation to help stabilise economic and financial conditions.

But the combination of debt and deflation is a new ball game! Business managers have to replace their focus from one of being paid more by growing the business to being paid more by contributing to shareholder value. With debt deflation limiting growth and pricing power, they will have to focus on cost-cutting. In the 1990s, the trend was to cut costs through the use of information technology and other capital goods. That seemed to work as the production of capital goods and the investment in technology added more than enough jobs to offset the loss of jobs as capital replaced workers. However, the prolonged new era of lack of pricing power will eventually drive corporates to focus cost-cutting not only on eliminating jobs but also on saving money in the capital goods sector. This may in fact be happening since 2000, as the US economy entered a recession not because of rising inflation that triggered a monetary tightening by the Federal Reserve, but because of a sharp reduction in capital goods investment. What all this means is that debt-deflation is inflicting a negative shock on global investment that could curb demand growth for a long time.

The unleashing of deflationary pressure from Asia after the 1997/1998 regional financial crisis has also changed the pricing environment. The competitive stress from China, growth drag from Japan, and excess supply pressure from Asia and elsewhere will continue to erode global pricing power. This means that inflation is not going to be a problem going forward. Indeed, the global economy has too little, but not too much, inflation for the first time since the Great Depression in the US. In other words, deflation and the resultant wealth destruction will replace inflation as the financial monster in the coming years. Even without deflation, subdued inflation may not necessarily mean economic calm, as the experience in the 1980s and 1990s has shown.

The economic and financial volatility of Japan's borrowing binge in the 1980s and of American's economic bubble in the 1990s both occurred in periods of low inflation. Their experience shows that price stability did not remove economic booms and busts. In fact, non-inflationary growth in the 1990s might have encouraged the excessive optimism that underlined the debt build-up. Stable prices, which used to be seen as a virtue, have backfired, prompting investors and consumers to form unrealistic expectations about future profits and income growth. The hype has, in turn, encouraged them to mortgage future earnings for excessive current spending. But central banks' focus on inflation fighting has prevented the authorities from realising that the explosion of debt had fueled asset price inflation in the face of stable goods prices. These financial excesses will have to be worked off. To minimise the negative impact on the economy, the purge process will have to be gradual, thus dragging global, notably US, growth for a much longer period of time than many people would expect.

A New Pricing Game

Therefore, Asia is facing a disinflationary environment, with deflationary traps emerging at times, in its economic transformation. But these secular forces may not necessarily always dominate just because they are ominous and grow over time. There are also powerful cyclical forces at work, which will dictate short- and medium-term economic trends. These cyclical forces will work at times against the secular forces, producing sunny spots for the regional economies. In other words, the outlook for Asia's economic transformation is not all that pessimistic. There will be periods of cyclical upturns within the secular downtrend that dominates Asia's economic paradigm in the coming years. Technically, what Asia will likely see going forward is a series of mini-economic cycles, with each cyclical peak lower than the preceding one. This "descending peak" pattern will form a secular falling trend, implying a structural downward shift in the regional growth rates.

Rapid productivity gains in the rich economies and intensifying competition from Chinese and Asian manufacturers have eroded global pricing power. This phenomenon will continue as China flexes her production muscles, unleashing more deflationary pressure. As a result, Asia will face a long-term decline in tradable goods prices during its economic retrenchment process. Crucially, improvement in technology will lower information and transaction costs, and thus intensify the tradable goods price squeeze. The technology effect will combine with China's impact to force a change in the nature of business competition. In particular, the tradable goods sector will become increasingly "commoditised". This means that for many tradable goods, product differentiation would be negligible and there would be numerous suppliers competing for limited business. This is equivalent to moving towards perfect competition where better and cheaper information deprives manufacturers of pricing power and eliminates their profit margins.

A prolonged period of falling goods prices could develop, just like what happened in the 1880s. Back then, the emergence of Germany, France, and notably the US as new industrial powers, due to rapid advances in transport technology (rail and steamship), had pushed down global consumer prices in the last two decades of that century. But in the new economic era, this may not be all bearish for businesses because higher income and rising consumer prosperity resulted from rising global trade will underpin prices of non-tradable goods, such as services. In other words, a dichotomised pricing game could emerge in the new paradigm, with falling tradable goods prices diverging from rising non-tradable goods prices. This pricing divergence will reflect the global economy's income gains driven by productivity increase and trade specialisation. Indeed, this price divergence is already happening in Asia (excluding Japan) and even in the US.

As evident in Figure 8.1, which shows the ratios of tradable to non-tradable goods price indices in Asia and the US, non-tradable prices have been rising steadily and faster than tradable prices since the early 1990s.

More interestingly, the pricing divergence is larger in Asia than in the US, as seen in the steeper rise of the ratio for Asia in the figure. This indeed reflects the more rapid income gains by Asian economies, which support stronger non-tradable pricing power, and the deflationary pressure that they exert on export prices, which erodes tradable goods pricing power, since the 1990s. Hong Kong is an interesting case in point. Deflationary pressures have plagued the territory since 1998. Even in 2002, five years after the Asian crisis, Hong Kong's consumer prices were still falling at an average annual rate of over 3%. Reflecting this goods price deflation is the territory's chronic decline in retail sales, which dropped by a cumulative 13% in volume terms between the onset of the Asian crisis and 2002. However, despite high unemployment and poor demand growth, Hong Kong has accumulated a vast amount of wealth, thanks to the benefits of international trade, the pillar of its economic growth. The wealth cushion has, in turn, underpinned spending on consumer services (not included in the retail sales calculation), which rose by 15% in volume

Figure 8.1 Non-Tradable to Tradable Price* Ratios

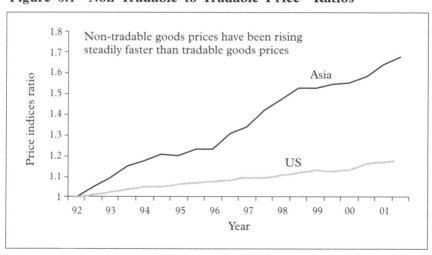

* Consumer price indices: 1992 = 100

between 1998 and 2002. The territory's divergence between the consumption of tradable goods and non-tradable services reflects precisely its divergence between falling goods prices and rising services inflation.

In general, this divergence between goods and services prices will remain, or even intensify, along with globalisation in the new economic paradigm. The rise of China and Asia (excluding Japan) as the world's manufacturing centres is a big supply shock for the global system. In particular, the importance of the rise in China's economic clout in shaping Asia's transformation process does not lie only in intensifying competition and curbing pricing power. Coupled with market liberalisation reforms elsewhere in Asia, the China factor has also hastened global specialisation by driving the world's manufacturing activity towards the low-cost Asian economies. This stronger need for global specialisation arises because rich economies are facing persistent competitive pressure to sustain economic growth by shedding labour intensive and low value-added manufacturing businesses. Those who remain stubbornly in their old economic models and fail to adapt, like Japan, will suffer prolonged price deflation, currency weakness, and economic decline.

Intensifying global specialisation also means that rich economies might need to shrink the tradable goods sector and focus on services and high value-added output. It is thus conceivable that in a new global equilibrium, rich economies would run persistent current account deficits, which could be large at times, as they import most of the tradable goods from Asia to cater for consumption, backed by high income at home. This is probably why the US current account deficit had failed to correct throughout the economic recession in 2001 and 2002, a significant difference from past recessions.

Thus, with regard to production growth, low-cost Asian manufacturers will benefit from continued globalisation. Output growth of the goods sector will recover robustly during periods of cyclical economic upturn. But from the view of earnings growth, profits will remain compressed under deflationary pressures and massive competition, especially from the mighty Chinese manufacturers. This means that Asia's export-oriented growth model will become unprofitable, as erosion of pricing power will translate into less profit over time for any given volume of exports.

But Asia's services sector will benefit from rising consumer prosperity. Rising services inflation will help profitability in the non-tradable sector, so that value-added services such as wealth management, health care, logistics, telecom, marketing, advertising, and business consulting will retain pricing power. All this means that Asian economies would have to switch to a consumption-based growth model to generate more internal momentum and focus more on services and high value-added output. But this transformation is by no means smooth, as insufficient reforms and competitive pressure from China will combine to inflict a painful experience in the regional economies at the onset of the new economic paradigm.

More Productivity, Less Profits

For those who still think strong productivity gains will lead to strong profit growth, they will be disappointed. Even if Asian economies continue to restructure and trim costs, the resultant productivity gains may not automatically deliver growth in robust profits for quite some time. This is because there has been a structural shift in the distribution of profits from producers to consumers, thanks to the IT revolution. Rising competitive stress from China and constrained demand growth will only prolong this structural shift in profit distribution, resulting in a profitless recovery in output. The strong positive correlation between faster productivity growth and higher profits in the past 50 years has broken down since the late 1990s.

This is notably seen in America, where the US government produces some economy-wide profits data for analysis. As HSBC (a global bank) research noted, US corporate profits used to correlate closely with the changes in non-farm manufacturing productivity, especially during the 1980s (see Figure 8.2). But that was no longer true during the 1990s; and since 1997, corporate profit growth and productivity gains have gone opposite ways. Between 1997 and 2002, US non-farm productivity grew by an annual average of 2.7%, while corporate profits nudged ahead by less than 0.5% a year. The divergence

Figure 8.2 US Profits–Productivity Divergence

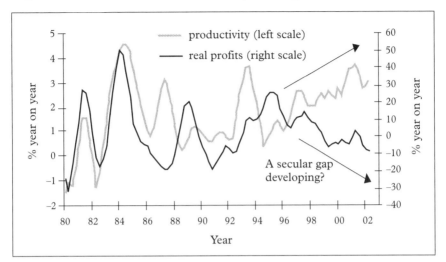

is more pronounced since 2000, when productivity grew by an average of 3.1% a year but corporate profits fell by 3.8% on average each year.

This "more-productivity-less-profits" phenomenon is likely to prevail in Asia as well, if it has not arrived yet. This is because the fundamentals behind the productivity-profits divergence are the same for Asia as they are for the US. The problem in the US is that workers, have received the bulk of this productivity gains in the form of rising real (inflation-adjusted) wages while companies' pricing power have been capped. This is like redistributing profits from companies to workers, and hence consumers. The sharp fall in the prices of IT goods has accelerated this redistribution of income. Notably, the IT revolution that has spurred productivity gains in the US has also intensified competition across the global economy, reducing barriers to entry in almost every industry, thus improving price transparency and driving down consumer and tradable goods prices. All this has fed back to erode manufacturers' pricing power and to squeeze their profits.

Such a profitless environment is not new. Consumers reaped most of the benefits of productivity gains from previous technological advancements, from the advent of railways to electricity to cars, as lower prices boosted real income while the lack of pricing power squeezed profits. But this time, with increasing globalisation, any productivity gains will likely augment the deflationary pressures from Asia's excess supply and China's competitive stress. This will benefit consumers more than producers and make dismal profits performance a norm rather than an exception in the new economic paradigm.

Nevertheless, none of this refutes the overall benefit of productivity gains. But the failure of productivity gains to salvage profits under the shadow of China suggests that profit expectations built into Asian asset prices would have to be lowered sharply in the new era. This has a significant implication on Asia's economic transformation. In particular, Asia's traditional model of generating profits from asset trading will no longer be able to deliver fat returns.

To a large extent, Asia's business model typically builds on buying a commodity or property and then selling it for quick profit without any attempt to build a lasting brand or franchise. This practice is known as asset trading. As the Asian "tiger" economies started to industrialise in the 1970s and 1980s, China was just emerging from her long economic isolation she did not pose any competitive threat yet. Thus, the Asian tigers relied on their low labour cost and steady rising prices, including asset prices, to reap quick profits via asset trading. Companies like Hong Kong's Sun Hung Kai, the territory's largest property developer, and Li & Fung Co., a giant trading concern, and Singapore's OUB, one of the city-state's banking giants, built their wealth on flipping assets under an inflationary environment.

Asia's New Economic Model

However, the gradual rise in China's economic might since the 1990s, notably her acceptance into the WTO in 2001, has changed all this. The rise of a competitive China has taken away the Asian "tigers'" competitive cost advantage over the developed world. The Mainland's productivity gains and over capacity in nearly all export segments are spreading and will continue to intensify deflationary pressures across Asia and the globe.

All this means that Asia will not only see the lack of inflation for many years. It will also see the death of its traditional asset trading business model, as flat or falling prices make it an unprofitable practice. Economic reengineering thus becomes a means of survival in the new paradigm. Asia will need to fundamentally change its business model by switching from trading assets to maximising sales through brand-building based on some fixed assets. This business strategy, which is widely pursued by companies in the developed economies, is known as asset turnover (technically defined as sales divided by assets). Outsourcing and adding value will be of paramount importance in this reengineering process.

The hollowing-out process in Hong Kong and Taiwan (see Chapters 6 and 7) will become more common throughout Asia in the coming years. This is a form of outsourcing that often means moving plants to China or other low-cost production bases in order to cut costs. For example, over 50% of Taiwan's IT products are made in China, and Acer, Taiwan's best-known computer brand, looks increasingly like a Mainland company with headquarters in Taipei.

Outsourcing is also happening on the revenue side when companies diversify earnings by penetrating overseas markets. This shift is notably seen in conglomerates, such as Samsung Electronics of South Korea and Shui On of Hong Kong, which is striving to double or even triple their sales revenues from China in the coming years. Indeed, revenue outsourcing has become a trend as trade globalisation intensifies. China will continue to be seen as a crucial market by multinational companies, as the Mainland economy continues to open up.

More crucially, the need to increase value-added is transforming the soul of Asian companies. China acts as the catalyst for this squeeze for higher value in the production chain. Under their traditional business strategies, most Asian economies have focused on trading and support functions, such as low-level logistics and mundane administration. They have ignored and thus are weak at front-end intangibles, such as marketing, design, packaging, innovation, and management. However, the rise of China as the ultimate powerful back-end machine has completely altered Asia's comparative advantage. All of a sudden, the rest of Asia looks expensive relative to China, thus making exports less profitable for the region. This means that most Asian companies will have to switch to front-end, higher value-added activities to survive the Chinese competition.

The Asian economic model in the new economic paradigm will also have to shift its emphasis from export-led growth to domestic consumption-based growth. The region's chronic problem is saving and investing too much but consuming too little. The result is the build-up of a large capital stock that yields a very low return on assets. Thus, a natural correction to this excessive-saving low-investment-return problem is to save less and consume more. Parallel to Asia's shift towards more consumption, local companies will have to build strong brands and franchises to maximise sales and revenues over a given amount of assets. They have to de-couple production from the home economy (i.e., migrate to lower-cost production bases), diversify revenue sources, and climb the steep value chain. These changes may sound drastic for Asia, but there is nothing mysterious about China's impact on Asia's economic transformation.

Asian corporates are going through the same restructuring process that American and European companies went through in the late 1980s and early 1990s. In fact, many Asian corporate chiefs may have already started thinking about retrenchment to upgrade and differentiate themselves. The emergence of China's economic clout accelerates this transformation. It also sends a clear message to Asia's traditional businesses that the change is no longer one of ambition, to be taken at leisure, but one of survival, to be implemented at once. Some Asian companies have seen the writing on the wall and done something about their business strategies.

Hong Kong's property developers have taken a notable and aggressive turn in their asset trading business. Tycoon Li Ka-shing has expanded into ports, retailing, and telecom from his traditional property business since the late 1990s. His group owns one of the biggest supermarket chains and mobile phone networks with strong brand names in the territory, and operates cargo terminals both in Hong Kong and China. Some others are shifting their attention to the Mainland to raise revenues. Vincent Lo, who heads the Shui On Group, a mid-sized real estate developer, has stopped bidding for land in Hong Kong since 1993. He has turned to China for development. Over half of his assets are in the Mainland and he expects to grow them to 80% of his total assets by 2012.

The new Asian economic model on a macro scale ought to involve changes in the region's capital allocation mechanism. One of the obvious problems under the existing system is over-saving. This is seen in the low ratio of bank lending to bank deposits, which has dropped steadily since the Asian crisis. A low bank lending-to-deposit ratio shows that the region is sitting on a huge pile of liquidity without lending it out to generate business activity. This reflects not only the lingering effects of the regional financial crisis on loan growth, but also the lack of saving alternations other than bank deposits. If the region is to transform its economic model to meet the challenges in the new paradigm, savers must begin to channel more funds into bond and equity markets. Hence, development of a better capital market is of paramount importance to facilitate Asia to upgrade its economic model.

China – A Threat, a Catalyst, or What?

The discussion here has taken the approach that China is a powerful force in shaping Asia's economic transformation in this millennium. There will be winners and losers in the transition period. But nonetheless, China acts as a catalyst to effect changes in Asia that will lead to a result where everybody will be better off after the transformation is completed. This view contrasts with those who see China as a threat, hurting her Asian neighbours and creating chaos in the region as she stretches out to grab others' jobs, market shares, and wealth. Some others see China's collapse under the weight of her structural and political rigidities, pulling Asia down the black hole with her. While books that predict a collapsing China or paint an illusive Chinese dream have made it to the best-seller list, some of them are hollow with no thorough research. I would like to conclude my view with some discussions on China's ability to effect changes and how so many so-called "China experts" have got their readings wrong.

The basic difference between a positive China watcher and a negative one lies in their understanding of China's reform dynamics. It is generally agreed that China has many serious problems that cannot be resolved in a short period of time. Notably, these problems include a broken banking system, an inefficient state sector, a mounting pension liability, and a deteriorating fiscal book – the list goes on. Her entry into the WTO in 2001 has also raised concerns about the ability of the Middle Kingdom to honour its free-trade responsibilities, and survive economic reforms and a more open system at the same time. All these developments are ongoing events. Thus, a positive China watcher sees China's reform efforts to right these problems from a dynamic standpoint, by checking if Beijing is moving ahead to tackle the woes and if there are structural changes underway. To the positive watcher, China's problems are evolving and so are her reforms. It is no point identifying the problems, like calculating the Chinese banks' negative net worth, and declaring the system is going to collapse. That is reading Chinese reform from a stationary standpoint, by observing that China's problems are evolving but her reforms are not. This is what the negative China watchers are doing.

For negative observers, the combination of China's economic woes and the opaque and corrupt political system is a perfect recipe for disaster. But they are looking at an evolving China under a microscope, which may be tainted. The conventional wisdom that the words and actions of her political leaders are the most crucial determinants for China's development has degenerated into just conventional thinking without any wisdom. Things are changing, and the political, social, and economic agenda is now written for, rather than by, the Chinese leaders. Just consider the enormous changes since 1980.

There have been enormous economic and social progress. China used to run a non-monetary economy, using ration coupons, work points, political background, and the size and influence of work units to determine living conditions. Money had no function as a medium of exchange and a store of value under the old system. The government effectively determined the population's access to daily necessities and economic activities. Then, the reform process began in 1978 with agriculture under the late leader Deng Xiao Ping. It freed the majority of the population from its dependency on the government. The importance of the private sector has since increased by the day, with millions of individuals and family-owned businesses becoming the backbone of efficiency and wealth creation.

The growth of the non-state sector is of vital importance. The savings and income of the non-state economic units are crucial to keeping the feeble state banks afloat as the government restructures the banking system. Without growth of the non-state sector, bank reform will only lead to an economic collapse as the economic losses from the retrenchment process will not be offset by the income and employment growth from the non-state sector. Jobs created in the private sector help absorb some of the surplus labour resulting from state sector reform, thus easing the social and political strains caused by massive layoffs. Mortgage loans, that China's new entrepreneurs and middle class are taking out, are one of the few sources of low-risk, profitable businesses available to banks. Such businesses are crucial to facilitate bank restructuring by moving the banks away from their reliance on state companies to consumers.

All these changes are crucial factors in assessing China's risks and opportunities. Nevertheless, politics still the most important thing in China. Economies do not grow in legal and institutional vacuums. China needs institutions, and only politicians can establish the institutional foundation. So, we may expect the political front to heat up in the coming years as economic reform intensifies. We may see some rough times in the Middle Kingdom, which will send periodic shock waves throughout Asia, as many Chinese still do not want to tackle the hard issues. But on the other hand, we may also see positive changes powering head, as those who understand the need for change consolidate their political power. The point is that it is too myopic to conclude a collapsing or rising China just based on some stationary factors and anadotes in the system.

As for those suspicious souls who fret about China as a major threat to Asia, they should not exaggerate the fears. The perceived "China threat" will likely prove to be similar to what hindsight told us about the perceived "Japan threat" in the 1980s. As investment bank Goldman Sachs once argued, the fear that China's gigantic size would crush the region by sweeping away jobs and foreign market shares is flawed. China is not that big in relative terms. Although China accounts for 20% of the world's population, her output is only 3.5% of the world's GDP and only 4% of total global trade value. At an annual income of US$900 per head, China is far from achieving superpower status that would threaten the globe.

China's total goods and services output is only 25% of Japan's, and 10% of Europe's and the US. The collective GDP of the rest of Asia is still larger than China's. As of 2001, China's GDP was about the same as that of Italy and France put together, and smaller than that of Germany or the UK. While China's foreign trade volume is larger than her relative GDP numbers, her foreign trade turnover is still less than Japan or the Asian Pacific economies in aggregate, and only 25% the value of the US's or the EU's external trade. Hence, China's threat to the global economy is far from justified.

There is no doubt that China's production and trade clout is rising. However, overall economic might is measured not only by output capacity and trade, but also the strength of financial markets. It is obvious that China is lagging far behind in this area. The size of the Middle Kingdom's stock market is a fraction of Japan's and smaller than the combined size of the other Asian exchanges. It is peanuts when compared to the giant US and European markets. China's monthly foreign exchange turnover is miniscule and barely noticable in regional exchange trades. Meanwhile, the Chinese renminbi, or yuan, is years away from being an international hard currency.

China's fast and steady growth record is often cited as a fear factor for many Asian neighbours. But look further into the regional experience, China's growth record is not that threatening. The Chinese economy has basically followed a growth path common to other Asian economies. Indeed, she has not come close to matching the stamina of Japan or the Asian newly industralised economies, or NIEs (the Asian "tigers" plus ASEAN) at their peak growth. For example, between 1970 and 2001, China recorded a four-fold jump in world trade share from 1% to 4%. While that looks impressive, the performance of Japan and the NIEs is equally strong with their share in global trade surging four-fold from 2% to 8% during the peak of their previous 30-year growth period. China's share of global output rose from less than 2% to 3.5% during the same period. But this rise was not as dramatic as the rise in the NIE's aggregate output share from 1% to 5%. And it is nowhere near Japan's record ten-fold surge from 1% to over 10%. The point is that if Asia, and the world, survived the rise of Japan and the Asian NIEs, there is no reason to fear that the rise of China will crush the other systems.

Finally, China's rapid export penetration into the global market does not necessarily herald the demise of regional trading nations. Indeed, China's trade performance is a natural result of her integration into the global economy. In the 1980s, capital and intermediate goods were shipped from Japan to Asia for processing before reexporting to their final markets. The opening of the Chinese economy has extended the intra-regional trade link. Many capital and intermediate goods are now shipped from Japan to Asia, notably the four Asian "tiger" economies, which in turn ship parts to China and the less-developed Southeast Asian economies for processing and assembly before reexporting to their end markets.

As a result, intra-regional trade with China has soared – a benefit for Asia. But being at the tail-end of the intra-regional production chain, China also records large jumps in exports, as goods leave the Middle Kingdom for their final destinations after being processed. This is a crucial reason for China's rapid export market penetration since the 1990s. Meanwhile, those economies that used to ship directly to end markets now see a redirection of their trade to China and other cheap production bases in Southeast Asia, giving an impression that their market penetration has dropped. But this is just not true.

In the thick of the smoke, what should we be looking at? Is China going to collapse or is she going to take over the world? There is no point jumping to conclusions by focusing on a few anecdotes because there are always factors to the contrary. Hard-hitting, sweeping judgments about China do not necessarily shed any light on reading the vast, complex China without robust research underpinning. In looking for answers to China's future and her impact on Asia, the appropriate approach is to avoid preconceived ideas, especially anecdotal evidence that one comes across in dealing with China. This is because one's experience of China may not be all there is to know about her.

The search for an answer must begin from a dynamic standpoint, as discussed above, by looking at China's key strengths and weaknesses, and the real issues facing the leadership. The Mainland's key strengths are:

- a strong reform resolve;
- a competitive edge in manufacturing, with improving labour skills;
- a large domestic consumer market that is starting to fulfill some of the perceived potentials that investors have been longing for;
- a resilient and growing private sector which is still constrained by access to capital; and
- a liberalisation process that is improving transparency and competition, thanks in part to the WTO membership.

On the other hand, China's key weaknesses are:

- her inadequate legal and judicial systems;
- corruption;
- shifting rules of the game;
- the cost and slow pace of financial reform; and
- an insufficient social security system.

The challenges posed by these weaknesses are formidable, especially the banking woes. They are not likely to be resolved easily in the short-term. There are few answers to these structural woes, but difficult trade offs that will create winners and losers. The government's role is to strike a balance between the winners and the losers so that the latter will accept changes. China is trying to achieve this without the formal democratic system that many analysts have been arguing for.

China's often opaque polities and corruption are not the whole picture that many critics painted. In some major cities, like Shanghai, some of the courts are improving. A growing middle class and private corporate sector are becoming more assertive in defending their rights and holding local authorities and commercial agencies to acceptable standards. Some non-profit organisations are working towards improving the credibility of elections in villages and townships, without the objection of the central government. These developments are spreading, although slowing. The lack of government intervention seems to suggest that they would become unstoppable social and political trends. They also show that the relationship between the people and the authorities in China had changed, and would continue to change.

So, will China rectify her problems or be overwhelmed by them? The developments in the past decade suggest that the Middle Kingdom's reform dynamics would remain positive. Its influence in Asia to shape the regional economic transformation will only increase through the years. The rise of China could either mark the beginning of a new Asia, or it could herald the end of an old one. In other words, the ball is in Asia's court whether it wants to exploit the opportunities offered by China and grow with her, or to stand back and be marginalised by the Middle Kingdom.

Index

Argentine peso and HK dollar peg, 126–127
ASEAN, 17, 54, 67–69, 75–77, 180
Asian banking system
asset management companies, 34, 35, 48, 85
traits, 14
Asian crisis
causes and catalyst, 8–10
crony capitalism, 9,15
economic transformation, 69
hot money, 16
moral hazard, 9
renminbi (RMB) devaluation, 70–75
structural problems, 9
Asian growth model
capital allocation mechanism, 177
consumption-based, 172, 176
export-oriented, 171, 176
Japan, 158
re-engineering, 174, 175
asset bubble, 16, 17, 26, 33
asset management companies
bad debt warehouse, 34,35
China and Japan, 85
Indonesian Bank Restructuring Agency (IBRA), 36, 41
Taiwan, 148
asset trading, 136, 174, 176
asset turnover, 175

bad debt warehouse
Asia, 34
Japan's RCC, 104

balance-sheet mismatch, 17–18, 77
banking reform
Japan, 101
Resolution & Collection Corporation (RCC), 103–105
beggar-thy-neighbour policy, 111
BIBF, 15
BIS, 94, 105
Bumiputra Policy, 40

capital account, 106, 113
capital flow and Asian crisis, 16
China
capital and currency accounts, 106
fiscal deficit, 84–85
growth engine for Asia, 63–64
push for reform and cooperation, 66–69
sequencing for reform, 106
source of deflation, 114, 169, 174
threat, 107, 108, 177, 180
China–ASEAN Free Trade Area (CSFTA), 67–69
China watcher, 177–178
Chinese fear and reform, 106–108
Chinese magnet
diminishing returns, 89–90
foreign investment, 79–82, 106, 152
SE Asia, 87–91
Thailand, 88–89
trade, 75–78
Chinese thief conspiracy, 70–78
commoditisation, 153, 169

comparative advantage, 65, 68, 79, 83, 90, 91, 94, 159
competitive pressure
  Asia, 58–60
  IT and China, 56–58
  renminbi devaluation, 59
  World Trade Organisation (WTO), 58
  yen, 111–112
confidence crisis, 23
  Asian crisis, 23
  Hong Kong, 127–129
contagion, 22–23
contingent liability
  Taiwan, 151
corporate governance, 33, 121–122
creative destruction, 80, 87, 106
crony capitalism, 9, 15, 21, 33, 38–39, 46, 62, 122
cross-strait trade, 130–131
currency crisis
  essence, 11–13
  missed aspects, 14–19
  moral hazard, 19, 20
  yen-induced, 111
current account, 106, 112, 151, 171
current account deficit
  confidence, 20, 77
  dangerous signal, 10
  funding, 16
  surging inflation, 12, 112
  wake-up call, 11

debt burden
  asset management companies, 34, 35, 85, 148
  global economy, 26, 52, 161–162
  Hong Kong, 120, 123
  private vs public definition, 33
  structural flaw in reform, 31
  Taiwan, 149

debt-deflation quagmire
  global, 165
  monetary policy, 167
  Taiwan, 149
debt-equity ratio, 31, 32
deflation
  global equilibrium upset, 47–49
  Hong Kong, 118, 120, 124
  Japanese burden, 98, 105, 114, 166
  productivity, 52–53, 172–174
  real interest rate, 142
  Taiwan, 141, 145, 149
  wealth destruction, 45, 52, 114
  World Trade Organisation (WTO), 53
Deposit Insurance Corporation, Japan, 3
dichotimised foreign exchange market, 71
dichotimised pricing game, 169–171
diminishing returns, 89, 143
direct trade link, 130, 132, 134, 152
disinflation, 53, 110, 112, 160, 161, 165, 168

economic complementarity, 64, 65, 79
economic recovery
  short-lived, 26
  V-shaped, 27
economic transformation
  challenges, 158
  different modes, 155
excess capacity
  China, 54, 58, 77, 152
  crony capitalism, 39
  global problem, 26, 48, 120
  investment efficiency, 44–46
  post-bubble, 51–53, 111
exchange rate shocks, 10, 58, 112

expectations
  exchange rate, 12–13
  profits, 49, 51–52

financial disintermediation, 80,
  84
financial panic, 21–23
fiscal deficit
  Asia, 111
  China, 84–85
  fixed exchange rate, 11–13, 112
  global, 166
  Taiwan, 151–152
fixed exchange rate, 123–124
floating exchange rate, 112,
  123–124
foreign exchange risk, 18

global equilibrium, 47–49
globalisation, 171, 173, 175
government guarantee
  asset punting, 17
  moral hazard, 19–21
  too-big-to-fail policy, 15, 20,
    21, 157
  US Savings & Loan debacle,
    20
government-directed lending, 35
government-linked corporations,
  41–43
Government of Singapore
  Investment Corporation
  (GSIC), 78
Great Depression, 164, 165, 168
Greater China economy, 117

herd instinct, 22–23
holiday economics, 84
hollowing out
  Hong Kong, 60, 175
  Japan, 96, 97
  new economic paradigm, 109
  Taiwan, 60, 141, 151–154, 175

Hong Kong and Argentine peg,
  126–127
  corporate governance, 121–122
  debt burden, 120, 123
  direct trade, 130, 132, 134
  dollar peg, 123–127
  economic transformation, 121
  Home Ownership Scheme
    (HOS), 129
  liquidity trap, 118, 121
  loss of public confidence,
    127–129
  middleman role, 130, 134
  Monetary Authority (HKMA),
    126, 139
  outsourcing, 153–154
  re-exports, 130, 133, 137
  structural solution, 137–138
  system failure, 127–129, 138
  transport and logistics, 132–135
  US economic cycle, 127
hot money and the Asian crisis,
  16, 18

IMF reform pupils
  South Korea and Thailand,
    28–29
Indonesian Bank Reconstruction
  Agency (IBRA), 36, 41
Information Technology (IT)
  Hong Kong, 58
  outsourcing, 55–56
  revolution, 172–173
international trade
  capital account, 106, 113
  current account, 106, 112,
    151, 171
intra-regional trade, 109, 182
inventory accumulation, 81, 82
investment
  Chinese magnet, 79–82
  complementarity, 64, 65, 67, 79
investment efficiency
  Asia, 43–45, 62
  China, 54–55

Japan
  Asian growth model, 158
  banking reform, 101
  Chinese fear, 107–108
  Deposit Insurance Corporation,
    103
  Financial Services Agency
    (FSA), 101
  hollowing out, 96–97
  Japanese threat, 107
  Koizumi, 100–102
  protectionism, 83
  reform failure, 82, 86, 97,
    100–105
  Resolution and Collection
    Corporation (RCC),
    130–105
JETRO, 88

Koizumi, 100–102
Korea
  cheating on reform, 31–32
  cost of capital, 33
  reform, 28–29

liquidity trap
  Hong Kong, 118, 121
  Taiwan, 141–142
loan loss coverage, 146
loan maturity mismatch, 17–18

Manulife saga, 36–38
middleman role, Hong Kong,
  130, 134
monetary policy
  flexibility, 13
  deflation, 163, 166–167
money velocity, Taiwan, 142–143
moral hazard, 9, 14, 19–21

negative net worth effect,
  Hong Kong, 23

net national income from abroad,
  97
new economic paradigm
  challenges, 158
  cooperation, 69
  debt deflation, 51–53
  defining characteristics, 7, 50,
    53, 161
  economic complementarity,
    64–65
  globalisation, 172
  hollowing out, 60, 109, 141,
    151–153
  painful transition, 8
  post-bubble adjustments, 165
  price divergence, 169–171
newly industrialised economy
  (NIE), 75–77, 180–181
non-performing loans
  Asia's burden, 33, 45
  dodgy definition, 16
  Taiwan, 145, 147, 150
North American Free Trade
  Agreement (NAFTA), 60

outsourcing
  Hong Kong, 153–154, 175
  IT, 55–56
  Japan, 97
  revenue, 175
  Taiwan, 153, 175

perfect competition, 169
political patronage, 39
portfolio flows and asset bubble,
  16
post-bubble transformation
  adjustments, 164
  debt deflation, 51–53
  investment, 50
pre-Asian-crisis growth
  tiger economies, 8
  TIM economies, 8

productivity and profits
   structural shift, 172–173
profitless economic recovery, 45,
   172
protectionism
   Japan, 55, 83

qualified foreign institutional
   investors (QFII), 151
Quantity Theory of Money, 143

real effective exchange rate, 73,
   124
reform and restructuring
   cheating, 31–34
   China, 66–67, 69
   complacency, 66
   illusion, 30–38
   inertia, 105, 107, 157
   sequencing, 106
   Temasek, 41–43
regional division of labour,
   64–65, 68
renminbi (RMB)
   devaluation, 59, 70–75,
      113–114
   dichotimised foreign exchange
      market, 71
   swap market, 71–72, 74
rent-seeking culture, 39
Resolution and Collection
   Corporation (RCC), 103–105
Resolution Trust Corporation
   (RTC), 103, 104
risk aversion and reform, 33
risk premium
   definition, 29
   problems, 30

Santa Claus economy
   Hong Kong, 119
self-fulfilling prophecy, 13,
   21–23

short-selling, 11
structural reforms
   cheating, 31–34, 111
   China, 80–81, 106
   Chinese fear, 106–108
   crony capitalism, 38–39
   foreign direct investment flows,
      87
   illusion, 30–38
   Korea, 28–29
   measures, 25, 91
   Thailand, 29
specialisation, 171
swap market, 71, 72, 74
Switzerland model for Hong
   Kong, 135–139
system failure
   Hong Kong, 127, 129, 138

Taiwan
   Asian crisis, 140–141
   asset management companies,
      148
   budget deficit, 150–151
   commoditisation, 153
   contingent liability, 151
   current account, 151
   debt burden, 149
   Democratic Progressive Party
      (DPP), 147
   diminishing returns, 143
   economic integration, 155
   economic transformation, 154
   Financial Holding Company
      Act, 147–148
   g-south policy, 156
   hollowing out, 141, 151–154,
      175
   Kuomintang (KMT), 146, 147
   liquidity trap, 141–142
   money velocity, 142–143
   One-China policy, 156
   qualified foreign institutional
      investor (QFII), 151
   secular downward trend, 159

terms-of-trade shock, 143, 144
underground financial system,
    145-147
Taiwan Strait, 130
Temasek, 41–43
tiger economies, 8, 54, 117, 174,
    180, 181
TIM economies, 8, 15
TIM structural problems, 9
too-big-to-fail policy, 15, 157

V-shape economic recovery, 27,
    30

wealth destruction, 45, 52, 118,
    123
wealth effect, 117, 135

white elephant projects, 100
World Trade Organisation
    (WTO), 53, 57, 66, 87, 117,
    121, 130, 135, 141, 150, 152,
    153, 174, 178, 182

yen's impact on Asia
    fading influence, 95, 96
    renminbi (RMB) devaluation,
        113
    weak yen, 93–95, 110–112

zero interest rate policy
    Japan, 99
zigzigging policy
    Hong Kong, 128, 129